Making

Right

Turns in

Your Relationship

Making *Right* Turns in Your Relationship

Myron D. Lewis, M.S.W.

 Hansyd Publishing

 Hansyd Publishing

First Edition 2004
Printed in the United States of America
Cover design by Daniel Tollas

ISBN 0-9754896-1-5
Library of Congress Control Number: 2004107638

Lewis, Myron.
  Making Right Turns in Your Relationship: How Couples Work Together to Create Change, Enhance Intimacy and Strengthen Communication.

1. Marriage. 2. Relationships. 3. Communication. 4. Love.

Hansyd Publishing
P.O. Box 557
Harbor Springs, MI 49740
231-242-0682
www.hansydpublishing.com

To Lisa, our marriage, our friendship
& our children.

ACKNOWLEDGMENTS

Thank you to all of the individuals and couples who have attended my communication seminar, *Making Right Turns in Your Relationship.* Without your participation over the years, this book would not have been possible. I wish you all the very best as you continue one of life's most challenging and rewarding processes: building a healthy long-term relationship.

I would like to acknowledge the following individuals who participated in small group discussions or manuscript reviews: Kimberly Beers, Maria Blackmer, Arturo Carrizales, Laura Chamberlin, Jane Denay, Cynthia Frizzell, Yolanda Hardison, Donna Harper, Aaron Huizinga, Stacy Huizinga, Carrie Iverson, Marge Kessler, Tom Knoerl, Lisa Lewis, Diane Matthews, Susan McCloskey, Tina McKee, Deborah Rosenberg and Terry Tollas. Thanks, to all of you for sharing and providing your constructive criticism and feedback. Your thoughts, feelings and ideas were all valued.

A special thanks to Dan Tollas, who completed the typesetting and cover design. Dan, thanks for working with and assisting me through this unfamiliar and most enlightening process. I would also like to share my appreciation to Gregory Hardison, Helen Leithauser and Heidi VanPatten for proof reading.

TABLE OF CONTENTS

Making *Right* Turns in Your Relationship

Making Right Turns in Your Relationship

*"You are today where your thoughts have brought you;
you will be tomorrow where your thoughts take you."*

—*James Allen*

Modern society has experienced many incredible transitions over the years to reach its current level of complexity. More pleasures and opportunities are available to us than our forefathers could have possibly imagined. Today, we have reached the "Communication Age." Computers, the Internet, e-books, cell phones, pagers, global positioning satellites, video phones and other electronic devices have changed our lives forever. We can collect, analyze, synthesize and share information at an ever-increasing pace. This has changed the format in which businesses run, market and grow. It has also impacted our personal lives. We e-mail friends and family, shop via the Internet, and use pagers and cell phones to keep track of each other. Soon the only place you will find a pay phone is in a museum.

Living in this new age of communication, it would be logical to assume this technology has brought with it advanced communication skills. Hypothetically, our relationships with our significant others (spouses, boyfriends or girlfriends) should exceed that of generations before us. Unfortunately, this is not the case. Technology has not made marriage or dating any easier. As a matter of fact, in many cases, one could argue it has made them even more challenging. You can count on many more advances in technological communication in the future; however, your interpersonal communication skills will be left for your discovery and development.

Many years ago, when my wife, Lisa, and I were dating, we realized that our relationship's future would be determined by the choices we would make individually and collectively. Even though we were both eager to build and maintain a healthy, long-term marriage, neither of us had received a solid education on how to do so. Considering our life experiences, this reality was a little intimidating. Lisa's parents had been divorced since she was six and my parents' success has been marginal, even though it has been long-lasting. As we looked around at our friends, families, co-workers and society as a whole, we recognized that we were not alone. For most couples, managing their normal challenges and emotions proves to be a true test of spirit and one for which we are not well-prepared. This will be the case if a couple is dating, newly-wed or has been married for twenty-five years. Neither Lisa nor I wanted our relationship to be a chance encounter. We wanted it to be an intentional, rewarding and fulfilling experience.

To more effectively understand the nature of healthy relationships and to become a better partner myself, I began searching out information on the subjects of marriage, love, communication, problem-solving, negotiation, decision-making, conflict-management, self-esteem, team-work, goal-setting and many others. After completing my Master degree in Social Work, I worked as a counselor and continued teaching the couple's communication course that I had begun developing while in graduate school. This book is a combined result of this knowledge and a reflection of my experience as a counselor, teacher, father and husband.

Valid photo ID required for all returns, exchanges and to receive and redeem store credit. With a receipt, a full refund in the original form of payment will be issued for new and unread books and unopened music within 30 days from any Barnes & Noble store. Without an original receipt, a store credit will be issued at the lowest selling price. With a receipt, returns of new and unread books and unopened music from bn.com can be made for store credit. A gift receipt or exchange receipt serves as proof of purchase only.

Valid photo ID required for all returns, exchanges and to receive and redeem store credit. With a receipt, a full refund in the original form of payment will be issued for new and unread books and unopened music within 30 days from any Barnes & Noble store. Without an original receipt, a store credit will be issued at the lowest selling price. With a receipt, returns of new and unread books and unopened music from bn.com can be made for store credit. A gift receipt or exchange receipt serves as proof of purchase only.

Valid photo ID required for all returns, exchanges and to receive and redeem store credit. With a receipt, a full refund in the original form of payment will

The next time you are at a restaurant, look around. You will see couples immersed in their lives. Some will be celebrating a birthday, anniversary, raise or recent success. Some will be enjoying a romantic evening or quiet get-away. Others will be struggling through a dilemma or challenge—trying to agree on whether or not they need a new car, or resolving an argument over how to keep the house clean or how to overcome tension at work, or grieving the loss of a parent. Given the right circumstances, the state of your relationship could reflect any one of these situations. The means with which you manage these various situations will strongly impact your relationship's long-term success.

When it comes to building a healthy relationship with your significant other, there are right turns and there are wrong turns. As a result of taking wrong turns, you will experience more tension, frustration and disappointment than necessary. The overall focus of this book is to avoid this by making right turns in your daily interactions with your partner. By focusing on thoughts, feelings and actions that support your relationship, you will be given more opportunities to accomplish this. Not only will you learn how to make more right turns, but you will also learn how to recognize and avoid wrong turns. As a result, you and your partner will experience more satisfaction and fulfillment from each other.

No one individual or couple is perfect. The truth of the matter is we are all doing the best we can with the knowledge and skills we have. This is equally true for your partner as it is for you. It is only by seeking new knowledge and learning new behaviors that you can improve the quality of your relationship. Regardless of intent, couples who fail to seek out new knowledge and behaviors are destined to repeat the same errors and will struggle to reach an acceptable level of emotional satisfaction. Whereas, those couples who intentionally seek out new knowledge and behaviors dramatically increase their chances of long-term physical and emotional satisfaction.

Through incorporating the lessons in this book, you will experience more consistent happiness in your relationship. The ultimate satisfaction, however, will come from reaching and maintaining a consistent state of knowing.

—Knowing that you and your partner will overcome whatever stands before you.
—Knowing that you respect, trust and appreciate each other for who you are.
—Knowing that you both feel safe to share, laugh or cry in each other's hands.

The confidence and reassurance that is achieved from this state is both overpowering and seductive. It is truly one of life's natural highs.

Today, Lisa and I have two beautiful girls, both of whom are sure to bring us a lifetime of challenges and opportunities. Yet, neither our, nor your, relationship's future success will come simply from good fortune; instead it will come from hard work, determination and a consistent focus on making right turns.

Getting Started

A healthy relationship is not something that happens to you; it is something you build and maintain.

One of the main objectives of *Making Right Turns in Your Relationship* is advancing your knowledge and personal communication skills so that you can achieve long-term rather than short-term satisfaction in your relationship. In order to get started, I would like to review the following topics.

✓ Characteristics of a healthy relationship
✓ Who is this book intended for?
✓ How to approach this book
✓ What if my partner is not ready?
✓ Making choices
✓ A couple's transition
✓ Turning challenges into opportunities
✓ Being the right person

Characteristics of a Healthy Relationship

Over the years, I have seen many couples struggle with the direction their relationships take them, rather than the direction they take their relationships. I have come to recognize that, although there are many ways to manage a relationship, there are common characteristics that separate those couples who experience success from those who do not. A successful couple has the ability to:

- Understand and respect their relationship
- Establish and maintain a relationship vision
- Make their relationship a priority
- Seek out and build interdependence
- Understand and develop emotional awareness
- Understand and manage their relationship's rules
- Use effective communication skills
- Work collaboratively to problem-solve and create positive changes in themselves, each other and the relationship

These fundamental characteristics apply to couples who have been dating for six months as well as those who have been married for thirty years. Over the course of this book we will cover each one of these topics in detail. As we do so, each chapter will build upon prior chapters until reaching a pinnacle in the last chapter. Alone or isolated, each chapter may be insightful, but it is their combined interaction and your actual implementation that makes them powerful. Couples who invest their thoughts, feelings and actions into the concepts shared not only experience more happiness, but others around them will see and feel it in them as well.

The healthier your relationship is, the more rewarding your life will be. This is not to say that happiness can only exist from within a relationship; rather the point is that your relationship should add to your level of happiness by being a source of strength, comfort and encouragement.

Personal development, along with knowing how to communicate and problem-solve, will bring you a long way towards a healthy relationship. Transferring these ideas into actions will allow them to positively influence many areas of your relationship, including, but certainly not limited to, your physical intimacy, emotional intimacy, spirituality, financial well-being and even parenting skills. Together, these skills allow you to manage whatever life throws at you. This does not mean everything will go smoothly in your relationship simply because you have practiced the methods in this book. Instead, these skills will give you an increased chance of successfully managing your relationship and life. Because of this, the content of this book is not intended to cover all the possible challenges you will face, but rather to give you a stable foundation to make decisions and act upon them, regardless of what stands before you.

When I ask couples, "What characteristics define a healthy relationship?"—they quickly identify the following:

Characteristics of a Healthy Relationship	
✓ Love	✓ Friendship
✓ Appreciation	✓ Fun
✓ Respect	✓ Patience
✓ Honesty	✓ Commitment
✓ Affection	✓ Determination
✓ Communication	✓ Genuine interest
✓ Listening	✓ Caring
✓ Understanding	✓ Attention
✓ Trust	✓ Laughter

When I ask couples, "What characteristics form an unhealthy relationship?"—they identify the exact opposite characteristics:

Characteristics of an Unhealthy Relationship	
✓ Disrespect	✓ Poor listening and
✓ A lack of appreciation	communication
✓ Dishonesty	✓ A lack of understanding
✓ Excessive arguing	✓ A lack of commitment
✓ Impatience	✓ No true friendship
✓ Limited fun, joy	✓ Resentment
or laughter	✓ Distrust
✓ Inadaquate affection	✓ Defensive
✓ Inattentive	✓ Nonsupportive

In every discussion about relationships, couples consistently identify "communication" as the reason for either a successful or an unsuccessful relationship. This seems logical, but it is not that simple. A healthy relationship means more than the word "communication;" it requires "action."

While people can easily describe what characteristics make or break a relationship, many have great difficulty identifying exactly how their behavior translates into these characteristics. Too often, our actions become so fundamental to our being that we lose sight of their impact. A good example of this is listening skills. In your mind, you may think you are listening, but your physical expressions, actions and words can tell your partner that you are not. In this case, it can be difficult to recognize your own behavior. This causes you to work against your good intentions. Yet, to be in a relationship that is conducive to good communication, you need to be aware of your actions and their impact. You can then choose to act in ways that support the characteristics of a healthy relationship. Overall, the deeper message of this book is to show you how to act more consistently towards one another so that the characteristics of a healthy relationship prevail.

Who is This Book Intended For?

This book is intended for men and women who want to actively manage their relationship's success. Therefore, it has equal value for couples whether they are dating, engaged, or married. All they need is an interest in reinforcing or improving their current level of physical and emotional intimacy.

Every relationship has its own unique challenges to overcome. This book simply shows how to apply basic concepts to actively manage the multitude of possible challenges couples will face. For instance, one couple may have step-children and another couple, biological children. Still, another couple may be able to procreate and choose not to while another couple wants children, but is unable. Each of these circumstances will place different stresses on these couples. However, the skills to manage them all remain the same.

This book is for those individuals and couples who do not want to passively sit aside as their relationship rolls forward. It is designed for those individuals and couples who desire new knowledge and skills so they can face the ever-changing landscape of their relationship and help cultivate its success.

How to Approach This Book

There are as many ways to read and interpret this book as there are people. In an attempt to meet different needs, I have included multiple opportunities to write down your specific thoughts, feelings and actions. This approach may be helpful for some learning styles and not others. For example, your partner may want to fill in every empty line while you may simply want to read it from cover to cover. It may come as no surprise that one partner may try to impose his or her learning style on his or her partner with intentions of helping the relationship. As a result, tension builds before the first page is even turned. Do not let this happen to you. If necessary, use two copies or write your comments and answers to questions on a separate piece of paper. This will allow each of you to read without being influenced by the other's written comments. Then you can share your thoughts and feelings in detail as you later review each chapter together.

I do not expect you to agree with every concept we will discuss. From time to time, you may strongly disagree with a point or an entire chapter. When this is the case, I challenge you not to dismiss the idea too quickly. Instead, I encourage you to put it aside for later consideration. Often those thoughts, feelings or behaviors that elicit the strongest reactions have the greatest potential to improve the quality of our lives.

As stated earlier, each chapter progressively builds upon another. As you read, questions will come to your mind that you will want answered. Continue reading from chapter to chapter and these answers will unfold. Once read in full, you will want to review individual chapters that you think offer the greatest benefit to your relationship.

What if My Partner is Not Ready?

It is not uncommon for partners to have varied opinions about their relationship's health. One may feel that things are just fine and the other may not. These different perspectives become more apparent when couples focus attention on their challenges. Initially, this can cause resistance in even the strongest relationships. However, it does not mean you should give up and walk away. You need not equate your partner's resistance with the level of his or her interest or caring. Again, it is often when we are the most emotional that we actually care the most.

A relationship does not change overnight. Each of you will take away different lessons, skills and objectives from this book and you will still disagree, get frustrated and struggle from time to time. For the most part, this makes you normal. However, if you continually get stuck, avoid conflict or always find yourselves imbedded in conflict, then you have not acquired the basic skills you need to be successful. Likewise, if your relationship has a deeper more prevalent problem like drug, alcohol, mental or physical abuse, then this book can serve as an excellent supplement to professional counseling, but it is not intended to be a substitute.

If your partner refuses to participate in the development of your relationship, then there is only so much you can do alone. However, by enhancing your own communication and problem-solving skills, you will reduce the intensity and eliminate many struggles your relationship would have otherwise experienced. This increased satisfaction is contagious and can lead a passive, highly independent or pessimistic partner to more actively participate in the communication and problem-solving process. As a result, your actions can positively impact your partner's behavior and your relationship.

Making Choices

The ability to become successful in our relationships lies in what we choose to do and choose not to do. Perhaps our biggest obstacle in being successful is ourselves. Our habits, personal characteristics, idiosyncrasies, and rules have a path of their own. It is not until we identify and understand them that we can actively begin to create new patterns in our relationships and do away with old unhealthy ones. Certainly, all people do not make good partners and all couples do not make good relationships, but a majority of us have a solid chance if we choose to work on building a stronger relationship. Whatever the current state of your relationship, the past is not the sole determinate of the future. You cannot change the past, but the future is in your hands and you can take it wherever you wish. As you read this book, you will be faced with many choices. What you choose to do with each of these choices will lead your relationship in a specific direction. Make sure you understand which direction you are choosing.

A Couple's Transition

All couples are faced with the transition of *bringing two distinctly separate sets of perceptions, beliefs, values and cultures together into a common, shared system, which supports the mutual needs, wants and expectations of each.* Those couples, who are able to make the transition, find the state of their relationship more manageable and rewarding. Those couples, who are unable to make the transition or who continue to struggle with this transition, find their relationship in a less manageable and more resistant state.

Making this transition is not as simple as it sounds. Learning how to understand differences and respect each other is a challenging task. Too often our own perceptions, beliefs and rules block our ability to acknowledge our partner. This causes a barrier of tension and frustration in the relationship, which prevents the mutual needs, wants and expectations of each from being met. It is not until both partners can move past themselves that they can begin to experience the true pleasure and excitement that their relationship has to offer. Reaching this state takes patience, hard work and determination. In fact, it is easier to fail in a relationship than it is to effectively build one. To undermine our relationship, all we have to do is not listen, fail to understand or grow. This approach allows us to demand changes of one another, rather than compromising or making changes in ourselves.

All relationships, no matter how perfect they may seem on

the outside, have turmoil from time to time on the inside. This is normal and should not only be expected; it should be something you are prepared to manage. Being married or dating is not so different from other relationships in your life. Think about it for a minute. Are your relationships with your parents, siblings, friends or co-workers perfect? I imagine not; likewise, it would be unrealistic to think of your relationship or marriage as a perfect experience or one that will just work out. Expecting perfection is not only unrealistic, but ultimately it will set you up for failure. Success depends on the skills you bring to your relationship and those you learn while in it.

Why or how your relationship started out is irrelevant. What you do to build and maintain your relationship is relevant. We buy life insurance, purchase smoke detectors and carry a spare tire, all in the unlikely event that something will happen. Unfortunately, many couples are more prepared for the unlikely event of a flat tire than they are for resolving their own relationship challenges.

You might find a compatible partner who has similar beliefs and values and enjoys some of the same activities, but you will still have differences that will arise and will need to be worked through in mutually satisfying ways. The ability to accomplish this through concessions, accommodations and compromises is significantly influenced by the individuals in the relationship. If a couple is unable to make concessions and arrive at agreements, then they are going to reach impasses. The purpose of cultivating a healthy relationship is to manage problems effectively so they do not grow into an impasse. This allows the couple to focus on the present and future, rather than being held captive by the past. Remember, it is not that which stands before you that determines your future. It is what you do with it that does.

As you work on building a supportive environment in which your relationship can grow, you begin to do so with the skills and knowledge you have acquired thus far. I believe this places many of us at a disadvantage because generally we receive minimal education and training on how to foster healthy relationships with our partners. Life offers us an informal education; this knowledge may or may not be helpful in our relationships. Think about it for a moment. How well are you programmed for success? I say, "programmed," because it is not until you understand who you are, what you do and your impact on others that you can actually begin to make conscious, uninhibited choices.

How Well Programmed are You for Success?

How well do I know and understand myself?
How have I learned to build intimacy?
How have I learned to problem-solve?
How have I learned to create trust?
How do my daily actions undermine my relationship?
How do my daily actions support my relationship?
What are my most important communication skills?
How well do I manage tension, fear, disappointment, and frustration?

One of the interesting elements of human nature is that we like the comfort of familiarity. We are more likely to continue doing what we know, even if the results are less desirable, than risk doing something different which leads us into unfamiliar territory. We are creatures of habit.

The good news is that we can learn new skills. The only limitations we have are those we choose to accept. Whatever your current skill level, if you have an open mind and are willing to expose your imperfections and take risks, then you can learn new skills.

Regardless of your differences, how you were raised or what you have learned, you and your partner both want the same things: *to feel appreciated, valued and accepted for who you are.* I have never met a couple who has reached this state and was disappointed. Similarly, I have never met a couple who did not overcome many obstacles in order to reach this state. It is okay for you to struggle in your relationship. Do not be afraid of this. Seek to move productively through your relationship's challenges, learning as you go, so that future challenges can be successfully managed with greater and greater ease.

Turning Challenges into Opportunities

I have seen many marriages end in divorce. Some were more surprising than others, but most were obvious outcomes of the investment. One couple shared with me that they had known their relationship had some problems, but never thought their challenges would lead to divorce, so they quietly ignored them. Unfortunately, it was not until after the marriage ended that they both truly realized the need to invest time and energy into their relationship from the beginning. As a counselor, I have seen and heard this story many times. For some couples, it is easier to trick themselves and avoid the obvious than it is to do something about it. Do not let this happen to you. From this moment forward, think of any problem, challenge or obstacle as an opportunity.

Opportunities allow you to make a positive connection with your partner by listening, understanding and respecting his or her thoughts and feelings. For example, I was once talking to a couple who had a conflict regarding how to store cups in the cupboard. He wanted all the cups open side down and she wanted them open side up. If he went to the cupboard and found them open side up he would turn them over. She would later discover this and turn them back. This behavior went on for some time and lead to several arguments. Then one day rather than simply disagree, they both took the opportunity to understand the reasoning behind each of their rules. He went on to explain that as a kid if the cups were open side up mice would leave little deposits in them. She had never had this experience, but once she heard this, she no longer felt compelled to keep the cups open side up. The impasse that had existed for this couple ended almost immediately just by taking the time to listen and share.

We all enjoy relaxing, tension-free interactions with our partners and the point of reading this book is to create more of them. However, you can count on problems continuously cropping up in your relationship. As a result, you are given the opportunity to confront and overcome challenges together. Each time you successfully manage this task the bond between you strengthens, your confidence builds, and you move forward with more determination than ever. On a different note, you could choose to think of every challenge as a barrier which prevents you from working together. Imagine the different dynamics between these two approaches, one recognizing challenges as opportunities, the other perceiving them as barriers. The perspective taken affects the very foundation of a relationship. Both building and destroying your relationship consume time, energy and hard work. What you focus on becomes the truth—it is your experience.

Being the Right Person

Your relationship is only as healthy as you and your partner. You cannot control your partner, but you can control yourself, and this can have a powerful impact on your relationship. You determine the path your relationship takes by the direction you lead it. Therefore, rather than focusing on what your partner is or isn't doing "right," focus on yourself.

28

Remember, you don't meet the right person; you have to be the right person. Your attitude is contagious. Is there someone you look up to? Chances are he or she has a good attitude. Likewise, your attitude deeply influences the overall direction your relationship will take. Everything you do, say or think plants a seed. Some of the strongest trees are those that develop the strongest roots. To build strong roots in your relationship, plant a positive attitude. Do not underestimate the power of a poor attitude, it will either bring your partner down with you or eventually repel them from you. In either case, the relationship loses. I have witnessed many individuals talking negatively about their spouses, boyfriends or girlfriends in a group setting. Often this is done in jest, but unfortunately, over time, what were once considered playful comments can create tension and undermine the fabric of the relationship. In essence, these comments reinforce a negative environment that will carry into future thoughts, feelings and actions. Think, speak and act enthusiastically about your partner, and make sure the attitude you project moves your relationship in the direction you want.

Your relationship is filled with many attributes, but there is a clear difference between those that are successful and those that are not. A healthy relationship is sure to exist when:

"Independence is equal
dependence is mutual
and the obligation reciprocal."
—*Louis K. Anspacher*

Seeking this balance is not easy. It requires hard work and an unyielding determination; however, in working towards it, you are more able to meet each other's needs, wants and expectations.

<u>S U M M A R Y   P O I N T S</u>

Whether you are preparing to take your relationship to a higher level or just want to get it back on track, you are choosing to invest in one of the most rewarding areas of life. It is through making many little changes, not big ones, that you will become better friends, lovers and partners. Like any other achievement in life, it takes time and focused energy to reach a goal. Both good and bad times will occur along the way. By focusing on personal development, healthy communication, and problem-solving, you are sure to build interactions based on trust and respect. Avoid taking your relationship for granted and work collectively to manage each challenge, for within each one is the opportunity to grow and learn from each other and to strengthen your appreciation for one another.

Self-Assessment Questions:
- ❑ What healthy relationship characteristics do I have?
- ❑ What unhealthy relationship characteristics do I have?
- ❑ Am I ready to turn my relationship challenges into opportunities?
- ❑ How committed am I to being the right person?

Moving Forward
Now that we have reviewed the basic premises of this book, it's time to discuss the necessary steps for *Making Right Turns in Your Relationship*. The first chapter, "Understanding and Respecting Your Relationship," demonstrates the importance of accepting four fundamental principles in your relationship. Once these principles are established, it will be easier to move forward.

CHAPTER ONE

Understanding and Respecting Your Relationship

"Destiny is not a matter of chance,
it is a matter of choice;
it is not a thing to be waited for,
it is a thing to be achieved."
—*William Jennings Bryant*

One of the first steps to *Making Right Turns in Your Relationship* is understanding and respecting the fundamental principles of a healthy relationship. When a man and woman come together, an invisible bond builds between them. This bond represents the emotional energy that ties them together. Even though this bond is not physical, it feels as if a rope has been tied between them. When negative energy exists, tension builds, the rope gets taut and resistance builds. On the other hand, when positive energy is invested, flexibility develops, the rope becomes less constrictive and collaboration follows.

The following four principles are intended to provide you with a strong base to grow your relationship from. By understanding and acting upon them, you are sure to increase your relationship's positive emotional energy.

✓ Every action is followed by a reaction
✓ For your relationship to win, you both must win
✓ Maintaining your love is a choice
✓ You cannot impose change on your partner

Every Action is Followed by a Reaction

The first fundamental principle of a healthy relationship is that every action is followed by a reaction. You and your partner are constantly influencing each other due to the emotional connection that ties you together. Because of this connection, awareness of how your actions affect each other is crucial. A key element of being in a relationship is not only recognizing and respecting your influence, but also acting appropriately with it.

As a partner in your relationship, you are both a teacher and a student. As a student, you are constantly being influenced by your partner's thoughts, feelings, and actions. If they are supportive and understanding, you will feel validated and acknowledged. If they are not, you will feel unappreciated or rejected. At the same time, you are also a teacher, constantly influencing your partner by your actions and reactions. If you are respectful and appreciative, your partner will feel appreciated and valued.

Think of this reciprocal interaction as an emotional ping-pong game in which you can either volley back and forth in a friendly match, or you can play to win at the cost of the other losing. Let's say your partner shares they are feeling overwhelmed with the combination of work, night school and the responsibilities that go along with raising two kids. What is your response to this self-disclosure? Is it to acknowledge how hard your partner works? Do you try to solve your partner's problem? Do you respond by focusing on your own problems instead?

Each of these responses is going to trigger a unique reaction from your partner. By choosing to acknowledge your partner's thoughts and feelings, you validate their feelings and let your partner know it is okay. Maybe this is all they need. But if not, you have set a supportive environment to assist your partner in problem-solving. By choosing to resolve your partners' problem, without listening first, you may save your partner some emotional discomfort, but you do not help them learn how to manage their own decisions. If you ignore your partner's thoughts and feelings and instead focus on your own, then you send a clear message that you do not care and that they are better off not sharing.

Think about this for a moment: What lessons have you been teaching your partner, and what lessons has your partner been teaching you? Over time, your interactions will lead to the development of relationship patterns. These are common interactions that build between partners and become second nature both in actions and thoughts. The questions to ask are: In what direction are your relationship patterns moving you? Are they pulling you closer together or pushing you farther apart? This reciprocal interaction is unavoidable in your relationship; therefore, you need to understand what you are accomplishing with your actions. Remember, every action is followed by a reaction.

For Your Relationship to Win, You Both Must Win

The second fundamental principle of a healthy relationship is that in order for your relationship to win, both partners must also win. Whenever there is a problem in your relationship, neither of you stands alone. You are on the same team. You are both part of the problem as well as the solution. This is not to say that no one is at fault, but instead that you both have a responsibility to solve the challenges that face your relationship. For this to happen, you must stand united and overpower the problems that get between you. If problems are allowed to drive a wedge between you, then you will begin neglecting your partner, your relationship and ultimately yourself. Keep in mind that "united" your relationship stands and "divided" it falls.

We have all, at least once, tricked ourselves into thinking we have "won" at the expense of our partner losing. In the short-term, this may feel good, but the long-term effect is more than discouraging. For instance, your partner misses the off ramp causing you to be late for your appointment. You respond by raising your voice, blaming them for not paying attention and then making an issue out of it the rest of the day. Another approach you could take is ignoring them by not talking and quietly fuming the rest of the day. In either of these responses, you have not only chosen to work against your partner, but you have also chosen to wreck the rest of the day. You could have easily chosen to make light of the situation, perhaps even reminding your partner of a similar error you made. Rather than letting yourself get upset, support your partner by letting them know it is okay. The choice is yours.

Remember, anytime your partner loses, your relationship loses, and as a result, you lose. Keep this in mind before you act on your next impulse. Consider the power of the choices you make and their impact on your relationship.

Maintaining Your Love is a Choice

The third fundamental principle of a healthy relationship is the importance of choosing to maintain your love. For many of us, love has always been perceived as fate, everlasting and withstanding the tests of time. At first, it just does not seem logical that we must choose to maintain love. Yet when you think about it, isn't that what commitment is all about? *Love can be elusive, exciting and complicated, but one thing is for sure: it is a choice to maintain.* It is your choice to act, think, feel and respond in ways that continually support your partner, yourself and your relationship.

You get to choose your partner. This is not the case for most of your other relationships; you cannot choose your parents, siblings or other family members. Even if you feel an irresistible attraction to another person, the choice to pursue and maintain love is still yours.

When love is not recognized as something that needs to be invested in, it is weak and easily corrupted by emotions. Your relationship will be awkward and unsteady at times because you will not always agree or understand each other. One of your best weeks together may be followed by one of your worst. For your relationship to sustain the natural forces and pressures it will undergo, love cannot be taken for granted. No matter how good your relationship is today, it will be tested tomorrow. When times are tough, your emotions will not guide you past the moment; your commitment will. Commitment is not only based on the love you felt yesterday; it is also based on the love you seek tomorrow. This choice is reflected in your actions to work together, to persevere through the bad times and take actions to create more good times.

When grown children move out of the house or go off to college, parents find themselves in an unfamiliar environment. For the first time, in twenty to twenty-five years, they are alone again. The house is quiet, there are no soccer games or parent-teacher conferences. For some, this is quite an appealing time. For others this is an extremely intimidating and emotionally frustrating time known as the empty nest syndrome. Why the dramatic differences in response to the same event? Some couples never stopped investing in their affection and attraction for each other, while others drifted apart as they fulfilled their own needs or got caught up in the role of parent.

We each enter our relationship with a unique set of needs, wants and expectations. The type of relationship you create is greatly determined by how well your combined needs, wants and expectations are met. Contrary to what many people believe, your relationship's success is not based on the initial love that was felt, but instead on how well you are able to maintain and build on that love.

Your relationship starts with love, but if neglected, love will not last on its own. The longer unresolved issues build, the harder they are to resolve. New issues take precedence, leaving old issues to build up even higher. Eventually, a glance or even the sound of your partner's voice triggers frustration or anger. When this state is reached, love alone will be unable to resolve the situation. Many marriages and long-term relationships fail simply because love is not recognized as something they must proactively maintain. By recognizing this choice, you take a mature step. By not recognizing it, you automatically put your relationship in harm's way. A healthy relationship takes time to develop and a lifetime to maintain. Falling in love is easy, but maintaining your love takes the knowledge to know how and the commitment to do so.

Initially, I found it ironic that it was not engaged couples who were most interested in my couple's communication course. I used to set up display booths at bridal shows so that young couples could sign up for the course. Yet, their interest was scarce at best. After all, they were in love and did not need any help! Instead, the appeal for the course came from older couples, some of whom had been married for twenty years and others who were entering a subsequent marriage. In either case, these couples recognized that a strong attraction, common beliefs and interests were not enough to keep their relationship vibrant. They knew that they had to choose to maintain their appreciation and respect for each other, through their actions, in order to maintain their affection for one another.

You Cannot Impose Change on Your Partner

The fourth fundamental principle of a healthy relationship is that you cannot impose change on your partner! Instead, change is accomplished by working together to reach mutually-acceptable decisions in your relationship. For instance, let's say your spouse does not like public affection or giving body massages that last longer than a few minutes. Yet, you are in favor of kissing and holding hands in public and enjoy giving and receiving long body massages. This variance in outward affection is going to cause turmoil from time to time as the needs of each individual collide. If no adjustments are made, then these differences will continue and cause long lasting tension. These adjustments do not have to be significant to be effective. Perhaps you agree to hold hands in public, but avoid kissing. As far as body massages, your spouse could agree to purchase you a few massages each year and build his or her tolerance up to ten minutes. It is through small compromises that partners learn to respect and adapt to one another.

On the other hand, when we try to impose change onto our partner we are greeted with resistance, resentment and avoidance. This is no different than how we feel when change is imposed on us. We all tend to be a little defensive and resistant to change. Therefore, it is only by working together that mutual change can be identified and carried out effectively.

Even though you can work together to change certain aspects in your relationship, you cannot change your partner's core personality. Nor can your partner change yours. Some of us process information at high rates of speed without delay, guidance or direction, while others process information more slowly and methodically. Some of us are internally focused and others are externally driven. Some of us are emotionally driven and others of us are cognitively driven. However, *even though personality is an important factor that must be understood and accepted, it is not the single element that determines who you become.* Your personality is a piece of the framework you perceive the world through. You can acquire new knowledge and learn many new skills to improve upon the quality of your life, but you will not change your core personality. You will always be better at some things and forever challenged by other things. You can take a shy person and send him through the best training in the world on public speaking, but he will never become as gifted and outgoing as an outward, charismatic person with less training. Therefore, there are some things that we need to accept in our partners and they in us. At the same time, there are many areas where we can work together to create positive improvements in ourselves and our relationships.

SUMMARY POINTS

Couples who understand and respect the dynamics of a healthy relationship are far better off than those who do not accept these underlying factors. Some partners cling to their beliefs in independence, without accepting the impact of their thoughts, feelings and actions on the relationship bond. This limited view unfortunately leads to poor decisions and actions, and the end result is often destructive. Keep in mind that your relationship is a delicate space that must be respected and valued. Understanding that every action is followed by a reaction can help you make wiser and more thoughtful choices and take responsibility for your actions. This in turn keeps you focused on the larger picture, your relationship, rather than just your individual needs. Hence, the focus is on both of you winning. Choosing to maintain your love with your actions will strongly impact the stability of your relationship over time. Finally, accepting your partner for who he or she is will save you a great amount of energy and allow you to work together rather than try to change each other.

Self-Assessment Questions:
- ❑ How do I support my relationship?
- ❑ How am I consistently accountable for my actions and their impact on my relationship?
- ❑ How am I committed to a win-win relationship?
- ❑ How have I chosen to maintain love?
- ❑ How do I try to impose change onto my partner?
- ❑ How well do I accept my partner for who he or she is?

As you consider the questions above, think of your daily actions, words, thoughts, feelings, gestures and overall behavior. Try to identify specific, yet common, behaviors that support your relationship as well as those that seem to undermine it. Once you have identified a few examples, I challenge you to observe yourself for a few weeks as these positive and negative behaviors play themselves out. It is often just by observing ourselves that we learn much about our behavior. This approach may seem very simple, but it has the capacity to create positive shifts in your behavior almost automatically.

Moving Forward

Understanding and respecting your relationship is a clear sign of making right turns. Now we will move ahead to discussing your relationship vision and how it allows you to stay focused now and in the future.

CHAPTER TWO

Your Relationship Vision

"Our plans miscarry because they have no aim."
—*Seneca*

Knowing where you are going is more important than knowing how you are going to get there. One distinctive characteristic of healthy couples is that they understand what they are trying to accomplish together. I call this a couple's relationship vision.

When asking couples what their relationship vision is, most respond with a questionable look, followed with the statement "to love each other and be happy." This response is vague at best. The purpose of this chapter is to help define what a relationship vision is, how it can help your relationship stay on track and how to create one.

✓ What is a relationship vision?
✓ How can your relationship vision keep your relationship focused?
✓ How to create your relationship vision

What is a Relationship Vision?

Your relationship vision defines the overall emotional connection you and your partner are committed to achieving together. It is that invisible connection of energy which bonds you and reinforces the beliefs and values close to your heart. Ultimately, this emotional connection is a reflection of how you consistently interact with each other. Therefore, your behavior and words will either move you towards or away from your relationship vision.

Many individuals and couples confuse their relationship vision with their relationship or individual goals. A relationship goal is something you want to accomplish together. For instance, having children, buying a house, keeping the house clean, going on vacations and saving money for retirement are relationship goals. Individual goals are more specific to an individual than to the relationship. You may want to eat a healthy diet, exercise regularly, build a workshop, complete your high school or college degree or become a master gardener. Sometimes, individual and relationship goals are combined, such as, both partners viewing healthy eating and regular exercise as important to themselves and the relationship.

The general assumption is that if relationship and individual goals are met, then the "relationship" will automatically work out. Certainly, these goals are important and are not something to lose track of, but your relationship vision represents the bigger picture. In other words, what's really important to give and receive from each other at an emotional level?

Virginia Satir, a well-known psychotherapist, put it best in her book, Making Contact, when she said:

> *I believe the greatest gift I can conceive of having from anyone is to be seen by them, heard by them and to be understood by them. The greatest gift I can give is to see, hear, understand and to touch another…*

In the process of life, we often forget what is most important to us. Your relationship is not just defined by what goals you accomplish together, but instead by how you consistently think, feel and act towards each other. How do you see, hear, understand and touch one another day in and day out? Your relationship vision therefore, is not something you can buy or place on a shelf. It represents the raw energy shared between you.

Your relationship vision focuses on the positive energy you want to experience with your significant other. When I ask couples what feelings and emotions are most important for them, they state that it comes down to feeling appreciated, valued and accepted. Achieving these is accomplished through healthy communication skills and behaviors that build on trust, honesty and respect. Unfortunately, there is often a disconnect between what a couple wants (to feel appreciated, valued and accepted) and how they behave. To reduce this discrepancy, we need to elevate the importance of our relationship vision so that it can help guide our behavior, especially when we disagree.

One way to do this is to sit down with your partner and define the overall emotional state you are striving for. Once this is done, you can convert this state into a still picture or movie that you can quickly refrence, to keep you on track. For instance, the following is the movie (visual picture) that Lisa and I created to represent our relationship vision. This description paints a picture for how we want to see ourselves now and far into the future.

> *We envision ourselves walking down a trail with lots of trees, flowers and wildlife. We are holding hands, smiling and feeling at peace with each other. There is a light breeze, the temperature is comfortable, the sun is shining and the sky is blue. As we look into one another's eyes we know we are safe, in good hands and confident that we will work together to overcome future challenges.*

Lisa and I defined this picture when we were dating. Since then, our lives have changed, our needs have changed, but the emotional connection we strive to fulfill in our relationship has not. It will never change; it is the same today as it was a decade ago.

How can Your Relationship Vision Keep Your Relationship Focused?

You can see from our example that Lisa and I have crafted a scene in our minds that depicts the emotional state we want to experience from each other. As a result, we have set clear expectations for each of us and our relationship. In order to reach our relationship vision, it is essential that we respect, share, listen to and support one another consistently. This means that some of our behaviors and attitudes will need to change as we seek to accomplish this. Certainly, each day, week, or month will not be as bright and blissful as we would like, but we are committed to move ahead with a defined purpose in our forethought.

Lisa knows that if I fall off track, I will need her help to get back on. She also knows that I am committed to our relationship and will take responsibility for getting back on track. This trust and confidence exists because we have earned it, not because we have not made mistakes. Our relationship vision keeps us on task by giving us a frame of reference—a standard to hold ourselves and each other accountable to, in the here and now. It is our commitment to each other.

With our relationship vision established, we can focus on our relationship goals. Lisa and I want a stable family income that will allow us to own a nice home, two automobiles, a boat or camper, vacations, as well as, save for retirement and our children's college educations. We also have many individual goals. For instance, Lisa wants to maintain a garden, learn Spanish or Sign Language and I want to write a book on relationships and volunteer on a community board. We both also want to stay active, eat well and exercise regularly.

It is important to keep an eye on our relationship and individual goals so that they do not overtake our relationship vision. In other words, neither Lisa nor I can work so much on building our careers or being the perfect parents that we sacrifice our time together and eventually our relationship vision. There may be times when relationship or individual goals take on a sense of urgency or additional time, but these situations are best if they are not the norm. I have seen many couples work so hard on their relationship or individual goals that they end up losing track of each other in the process. For instance, one couple shared with me that they had always wanted to build a cabin on some property they had purchased. As it turns out, the husband spent so much time building the cabin that they actually grew more distant from each other in the process. The cabin which had been so important to them actually became a sore spot in their relationship. Eventually to relieve themselves of this stress they sold the cabin and purchased an RV to tour the country.

How to Create Your Relationship Vision

Again, your relationship vision represents the type of environment and level of emotional fulfillment you desire from your relationship. To create and maintain your relationship vision, keep in mind the following basic guidelines.

- Develop your relationship vision together
- Focus on the emotional, physical and
  spiritual connection
- Write it down
- Review your relationship vision
- Reinforce what's working

Develop your relationship vision together

Take time to discuss and define your relationship vision together. Working on this together gives you the opportunity to share and reflect on the purpose of your relationship. If you are married, review your wedding vows. What do these mean to you today? If you are dating, what is it that you want to achieve together at an emotional level? Working together on your relationship vision is not only important, but it is something you both must agree to and be committed to, in order for it to be successful.

Focus on the emotional, physical and spiritual connection

How do you want to feel, think and behave towards one another? What is the emotional connection you want to build and maintain? Once you can articulate the emotional, physical and spiritual vision you seek, create a visual representation in your mind. How will you know when you reach this state? What type of expression would be on your face? How would you be walking? What type of thoughts would be going through your head? How would you support each other when things are not working out as you would like?

Write it down

Write down the various thoughts, feelings and actions that you believe represent your relationship vision. From this list, write a brief statement like Lisa and I have, which represents the positive emotional connection you both seek in your relationship.

Our Relationship Vision

_____
_____
_____
_____
_____
_____
_____
_____
_____
_____
_____

Review your relationship vision

Once your relationship vision has been defined, it is important to periodically take time to review how your actions have been leading you towards or away from your vision. That is, if trust is an important component of your relationship vision, how did you work towards that feeling the last time you had a disagreement? Completing a review several times a year is not only insightful; it is also extremely helpful. First, it will serve as a reminder to what you are working towards. This is important, because it is easy to get lost in the everyday grind. Second, you will recognize areas where you have not consistently chosen to support your relationship with your actions. These areas can then be resolved with communication and problem-solving skills, both of which will be thoroughly discussed in later chapters.

Reinforce what's working

Your relationship vision needs to be cultivated, fertilized and watered to become strong. Support your successes and strive to create positive connections. Positive reinforcement and respect can go a long way towards increasing recurring behavior. For instance, if your partner reaches out and shares something personal, responding with a warm smile, a reassuring gesture and a genuine "thank you" will go a long way towards increasing the likelihood that the behavior will be repeated. By not taking advantage of these opportunities, many couples undermine themselves. Rather than positively reinforcing their partner, they avoid it because they feel their partner should not be rewarded for behavior that is an "expectation." Unfortunately, this belief, regardless of any good intentions, will limit a couple's success and appreciation for each other.

Contrary to popular opinion, just because two adults agree on what they want to accomplish, does not mean they know how. Therefore, at times our actions will be incongruent with our vision. However, without vision, your relationship can become very confusing, and the last thing you want to do is leave something so important to chance. With your vision clearly stated, you have the ability to quickly recognize and respond when you have fallen off track. At any moment, you can compare your immediate actions and feelings to your relationship vision and determine if you are meeting your own expectations.

In speaking with couples who have defined their relationship vision, many feel that for the first time they have consolidated their various thoughts and feelings into a genuine direction.

Each year brings with it different trials and challenges, and, because of this, you can expect to be pulled off track. The longer you are off track, the more difficult it can be to get back on. Therefore, the secret for not falling off track too long is recognizing when you have fallen off and your relationship vision is an excellent means for making this happen.

Once established, your relationship vision becomes a permanent fixture. It is not a temporary agenda; its value is the same today as it will be in fifteen or fifty years.

SUMMARY POINTS

Your relationship vision underscores all the beliefs and values you hold in your relationship. It is a vision of what your relationship seeks to be at an emotional level. By creating it and holding your actions accountable to it, you are more likely to experience the level of emotional, physical and spiritual happiness you seek. Whatever your goals are in life, the clearer your relationship vision is, the greater your chances for success.

Self-Assessment Questions:
- ❑ What is our relationship vision?
- ❑ How have I let relationship or individual goals block our relationship vision?
- ❑ How do I use positive reinforcement?
- ❑ What is one thing I could do today to better support my relationship vision?

Moving Forward

Establishing your relationship vision gives you a standard to work towards. It is the building block from which your relationship grows. The next component to *Making Right Turns in Your Relationship* is learning how to make your relationship a priority by your actions.

CHAPTER THREE

Making Your Relationship a Priority

*"No question is so difficult to answer as that
to which the answer is obvious."*
—*George Bernard Shaw*

Consistently making your relationship a priority, day in and day out, sets a positive tone. In the movie, *What About Bob*, Bill Murray played the neurotic character, Bob, who is in desperate need of psychotherapy. One of the recurring themes of the comedy is the consistent challenge by Bob's psychiatrist to take "baby steps" towards improving his self-confidence. Over the course of the movie, through small humorous steps, Bob is able to slowly recover from his neuroses and regain confidence. This same approach, taking small steps, applies to many areas of your life and can dramatically enhance the quality of your relationship. Below are two simple steps you can take to make your relationship a priority.

✓ Set time aside
✓ Acknowledge positive characteristics and behaviors

These small steps are nothing new to most of us. Yet, it is amazing how often we forget about them or simply take them for granted. Contrary to popular opinion, what we know or what we talk about is not as important as what we do.

By setting time aside and acknowledging each other, our behavior reinforces a positive emotional bond in our relationship.

Set Time Aside

The importance of setting time aside for your relationship cannot be overstated. After all, it is your behavior—not your intentions—that will move you towards your vision and goals. The purpose of setting time aside is not to spend all your time with your partner or avoid spending time with friends and hobbies; instead the purpose is to create a healthy balance. Too often couples get so caught up in their children or work that they forget to give their relationship the necessary time and energy to keep it vitalized. As a result, the relationship suffers, and when children are involved, they too feel the negative impact. It is easy to deceive ourselves into believing the relationship will "just work out on its own." Unfortunately, nothing could be further from the truth. Make your relationship a priority by setting time aside.

You can rob yourself of many treasures, but do not allow time to be one of them. One thing is for certain: if you wait for time, you will never have any.

How satisfied are you with the quantity of time you spend together? How satisfied are you with the quality of time you spend together? If you are both comfortable with the quantity and quality of time together, keep up the good work. If you are still searching for a more comfortable balance, now is your opportunity to achieve it. Life can get extremely busy, and time can seem like a precious commodity. In order to get more time on your side, you will need to give up other things. This is not always easy. Television, sports, the kids, that night out with friends can all seem pretty important. Take this opportunity to understand how your interactions are supporting your relationship and how you can improve them by:

- Taking advantage of your daily interactions
- Taking advantage of your weekly interactions
- Taking advantage of your monthly interactions
- Taking advantage of your yearly interactions

Taking advantage of your daily interactions

Daily time is not necessarily about quantity; instead it is a reflection of quality. A passing touch, a good morning kiss, an afternoon hug, a love note slipped into a coat pocket, a genuine smile or a few minutes of solid conversation are all moments that impact your daily life. Looking for, creating and making the best of these moments will heighten your enthusiasm and attraction for one another. How have you chosen to touch your partner today? Identify a few behaviors you already do, used to do or would like to start doing as a part of your daily interactions.

> What behaviors would you like to start implementing daily?
> 1. _____
> 2. _____
> 3. _____

These types of behaviors are choices you make. By intentionally reaching out to your partner, you build positive patterns that reinforce respect, appreciation, value and understanding. Another way to improve your daily interactions is to avoid behaviors that cause negative thoughts and feelings, such as ignoring one another, turning away from each other when in conflict, being judgmental, demanding, condescending or disrespectful.

> What behaviors do you want to stop doing on a daily basis?
> 1. _____
> 2. _____
> 3. _____

It takes significantly more positive interactions than negative ones to keep your relationships balanced. Therefore, the fewer negative interactions you can create and the more positive ones you build, the better off you will be.

Taking advantage of your weekly interactions

I have seen this range anywhere from Sunday breakfast, going for Saturday morning walks, going out to dinner on Friday nights, watching a movie, playing a game or just setting time aside one night a week to talk. What do you do to set time aside weekly?

> What weekly activities would you like to continue or start?
> 1. _____
> 2. _____
> 3. _____

Some couples are so busy that weekly time together is often lost before they know it. When this is the case, taking advantage of those daily moments you have identified is irreplaceable.

What types of things could you stop or reduce in order to have more quality time together? Could you come home from work earlier one night? Could you watch less TV, read fewer books or participate in fewer social activities at work or with friends?

What behaviors do you want to discontinue or reduce
on a weekly basis?

1. _____
2. _____
3. _____

Taking advantage of your monthly interactions

My oldest sister and her husband are very good at this.
They have three children and demanding careers. As you can
imagine, their lives are very busy. However, one thing they
have always made time for is their relationship. They go to
dinners, movies or concerts throughout the year. They have
always enjoyed these activities and they have never let their
busy lives stop them from enjoying one another.

At the same time, we all know couples who do very little
together to keep the passion going. It's absolutely amazing
how a few hours alone can be very refreshing and enjoyable,
so long as you put the pressures and stresses of everyday life
behind you.

It is not necessary to keep track of each month's activities.
Sometimes a few months will tick by with few opportunities, and
at other times a week does not go by without having some fun
together. What activities do you do together on a monthly basis?

What monthly activities would you like to start or
continue dedicating time to?

1. _____
2. _____
3. _____

Likewise, it is important to identify any activities that you could stop doing that would allow you more quality interactions on a monthly basis.

> What monthly activities would you like to stop dedicating time to?
> 1. _____
> 2. _____
> 3. _____

Taking advantage of your yearly interactions

This may come as no surprise, but buying flowers or going out to dinner on your anniversary is not enough. However, going away for a weekend without friends or your children can be. Making plans for a special time together keeps you both focused and gives you something special to look forward to.

Before we had kids, Lisa and I enjoyed going on weekend camping trips. Neither of us could have ever imagined not going on these trips. Yet, once our children were born, we found ourselves so busy that we forgot about one of our favorite past times, camping. Life has a way of sneaking up on adults and robbing them of things that are important. Do not let this happen to you. Now, Lisa and I make it a priority to go camping together once a year with no kids or noise, just a campfire, our bikes and a deck of cards. What activities are you committed to on an annual basis?

> What activities are you commited to achieving on a yearly basis?
> 1. _____
> 2. _____
> 3. _____

As you can see, there are daily, weekly, monthly and yearly opportunities to set time aside, none of which require anything fancy or an extraordinary amount of time or energy in order to be effective. It is the combination of your interactions that will foster the healthy behaviors of a successful relationship. What do you think would happen to your relationship if you were to take many vacations throughout the year, see the places you have always wanted to see, but while doing so experienced very few positive daily interactions with your partner? That's right, you would have a full passport, but your relationship would be running on empty.

Some couples spend much of their time away from each other due to work. The military, corporate travel and sales are often responsible for keeping partners apart for days, weeks or months at a time. This, however, does not take away the value of making positive connections on a regular basis. The responsibilities of work may place them physically apart, but with today's technology it does not have to push them emotionally apart. Cell phones, video conferencing and e-mail make it easier than ever to keep active communication going.

Again, life can easily be made more difficult than need be. All you really need is a relationship vision and a willingness to act on it. Do not make it any more complicated—stay focused by setting positive interactions and time aside on a daily, weekly, monthly and yearly basis.

Acknowledge Positive Characteristics and Behaviors

The second part of making your relationship a priority is learning to acknowledge the positive characteristics and behaviors of your partner. Have you ever lost a friend or family member unexpectedly? If so—you have probably learned that often it is only after someone is gone that you fully realize his or her true value. Human nature, it seems, leads us to take for granted what we have and instead focus our attention on what we do not have. Part of being in a supportive relationship is avoiding this trap by consistently recognizing and acknowledging positive characteristics and behaviors in each other.

How many positive characteristics and behaviors can you identify about your partner in a minute? If only a handful of ideas come to your mind, do not be alarmed; you are not alone. Most of us do not store, at the tip of our tongue, this type of information.

For many years, I have had couples complete an exercise to bring forward the positive characteristics and behaviors of their relationships. I share it with you in hopes that it will touch your life as it has so many others. All you need is twenty quiet and committed minutes with your partner. The first step of this exercise is to identify positive characteristics and behaviors of your partner. In order to be successful, you will need to look beyond his or her imperfections and your own idiosyncrasies. To help you along this path, here are some examples to get you thinking:

Positive Characteristics/Attributions		
A wonderful smile	Soft skin	Beautiful hair
Caring	Supportive	Detailed
Hard working	Responsible	Considerate
Confident	Respectful	Appreciative
Fun	Positive	Determined
Relaxed	Optomistic	Loving
Passionate	Helpful	Attractive
Sexual	Honest	Humorous

With these examples in your mind, take a moment to identify several positive characteristics or behaviors that you appreciate in your partner.

Identify several positive characteristics or behaviors of your partner.

1. _____
2. _____
3. _____
4. _____
5. _____
6. _____
7. _____
8. _____

It may take you a few minutes to create a list, but once you have, you're ready for the second step: sharing your list with each other. As you share these positive characteristics, make sure you are sitting down, facing each other, and are in physical contact. This can be accomplished by holding hands or just sitting close together. To further enhance your overall communication, make sure to use eye contact and a soft voice.

As you share positive characteristics or behaviors use real examples to help illustrate your points. The following is an example of what this communication might sound like.

Characteristic: *You are very considerate!*
Example: *When I forgot my lunch last week, you took the time to drop it off to me on your way to work. That was very considerate, and I really appreciated it. Thanks.*

You will find out that sharing your list will not take long, but the impact will be powerful. I have seen many couples become tearful, hug each other and smile upon completing this task. As you will see, this exercise will quickly make you feel recognized, valued and appreciated for who you are and what you do. It will also validate your partner's thoughts, feelings and actions.

Upon asking couples how often they share at this level, the answer is almost always the same: "almost never." Sharing is caring, and its effectiveness can be enhanced dramatically when using a soft tone, eye contact and a gentle touch.

It is not necessary to create a list every week and share. Instead, the purpose of this exercise is to promote the activity of consistently recognizing and acknowledging positive characteristics or behaviors when they occur, rather than ignoring them or believing that reinforcing basic expectations should not be necessary. Always remember what you have and at the slightest opportunity acknowledge your partner by sharing your positive thoughts and feelings. This will give you more in return than any criticism will ever achieve.

So often, we wonder if we are doing things right; yet when our behavior is positively acknowledged, doubt is lost, and we increase the frequency of that behavior. Remember this as you approach your partner with your thoughts, feelings or behaviors. Each and every day is an opportunity to acknowledge your partner. It is through small emotional contacts that you build trust and intimacy.

SUMMARY POINTS

It is so easy to get caught up in the responsibilities, tasks and goals of everyday life, that we forget what is most important to us. A minute turns into a day and a day into a week, and before you know it a year has gone by. Making your relationship a priority sets a standard and makes it an unmistakable mission in your life. There is no better way to do this than by setting time aside and acknowledging your partner with positive affirmations. Each of these steps has a great amount of influence alone, but together they have a defining impact on your relationship's long-term success.

Self-Assessment Questions:
- ❑ How have we set the necessary quantity and quality of time aside for our relationship?
- ❑ What behaviors could I stop in order to create more quality time in my relationship?
- ❑ What behaviors could I start doing to create more quality time in my relationship?
- ❑ How have I chosen to acknowledge the positive characteristics and behaviors of my partner?

Moving Forward

Setting aside time and focusing on the positive makes your relationship a place of comfort. As we move forward in *Making Right Turns in Your Relationship*, the next topic will focus on creating interdependence in our thoughts, feelings and actions. In doing so, we can more easily reach mutual respect and appreciation in our relationship.

Making Right Turns in Your Relationship

CHAPTER FOUR

Creating Interdependence

Some people just go through life;
others choose to live life.

If there is any single characteristic, on which you can build, that will allow you to become a healthier partner, it is your level of "interdependence." Achieving a state of interdependence enables you to effectively manage the natural struggles and opportunities your relationship will face.

We all share traits of both dependence and independence in our personalities. The more balance that exists between these characteristics, the more interdependent we become. The greater the imbalance, the more difficult it will be for us to establish a healthy relationship. The goal of this chapter is to help you understand the following topics:

✓ Dependence
✓ Independence
✓ Interdependence
✓ Increasing your level of interdependence
✓ Understanding the type of relationship you have

Dependence

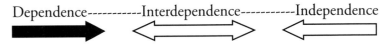

Dependence----------Interdependence----------Independence

We all entered the world wholly dependent on those around us. As infants, children, adolescents and even young adults, we depended on our parents to provide us nourishment, give us shelter and console our emotions. Dependence is a normal, fundamental aspect of life and as we age, learn and grow, the role it plays in our lives changes, but its value does not. In taking a closer look at dependence, it becomes evident that there are both healthy and unhealthy characteristics.

Characteristics of Unhealthy Dependence

Indecisive	Easily swayed
Constantly seeking approval	Afraid of conflict
Insecure	Always agreeable
Self-blaming	Unassertive
Uncomfortable sharing feelings	Passive

Typically when we think of dependence we think of its weaknesses rather than its strengths. However, as you will see below, dependence has many healthy characteristics, all of which we have identified as being fundamental to your relationship's success.

Characteristics of Healthy Dependence

Patient	Considerate
Caring	Understanding
Dependable	Forgiving
Easy Going	Trusting
Empathetic	Giving

What happens when an individual favors dependence?

As we have discussed, dependence is an important trait of being a good partner. When in conflict or making decisions, healthy dependence allows partners to listen and understand one another. For instance, take the following situation between Sue and Rob.

Sue: *You watch too much TV!*
Rob: *What do you mean, I watch too much TV?*
Sue: *As soon as you get home, you turn on the TV and it's on until you go to bed.*
Rob: *I do like watching TV.*
Sue: *Yes you do!*
Rob: *How about if I shut the TV off after the evening news.*
Sue: *That would be great.*

Because Rob favors healthy dependence, his reaction is to understand his partner and reach a compromise. If Rob had favored the characteristics of unhealthy dependence, this conversation would be completely different. Rather than trying to understand Sue, he would avoid any tension that would be created by differences in their thoughts, feelings or actions.

Sue: *You watch too much TV!*
Rob: *You're right; I should not take time out for myself. There is so much to get done around the house. I'm sorry to disappoint you.*

The level of our dependence, whether healthy or unhealthy, is determined by the underlying motivation of our thoughts, feelings and actions. For instance, is our desire to be considerate based on a lack of self-confidence and a constant need for approval, or does it stem from a state of self-confidence, fostered by a genuine desire to understand and respect others?

Independence

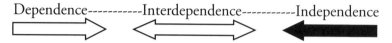

Dependence-----------Interdependence-----------Independence

Even though we are brought into this world in a complete-ly dependent state, we quickly begin building independence. Each and every day children develop more awareness and control over their own consciousness, bodies' functions and decisions. What we term as the "terrible twos" is clearly a time when children are actively exploring their world and taking more control of it. This growth of independence continues on into adolescence where they explore their identity and sense of self. This maturation further continues on into adulthood. As with dependence, independence also falls into two categories: healthy and unhealthy.

Characteristics of Unhealthy Independence	
Not empathetic or understanding	Selfish
Self-centered	Demanding
Over-reactive	Blaming
Intolerant	Argumentative
Impatient	Untrusting
Emotionally over-secure	Unforgiving
Disrespectful	

Many of us view independence as a sign of courage and strength as the characteristics below will show. Generally this is the case, yet the characteristics above undermine one's abil-ity to listen and work together. This can actually prevent one from sharing, growing and learning, all of which represent essential components of a healthy relationship.

Characteristics of Healthy Independence	
Able to make quick decisions	Willing to take risks
Not afraid to fail	Able to stand up for self
Able to say no	Passionate
Accepting of challenges	Confident

What happens when an individual favors independence?

Clearly, independence is an important factor in being a good partner. It gives us the ability to believe in and stand up for ourselves, as well as to face challenges and make decisions. Previously, while discussing dependency, we reviewed interactions between Sue and Rob. If Rob had favored the characteristics of healthy independence instead, their interaction would change:

Sue: *You watch too much TV!*

Rob: *What do you mean, "I watch too much TV?"*

Sue: *As soon as you get home, you turn on the TV, and it's on until you go to bed.*

Rob: *Well, I work hard and need a break.*

Sue: *So do I, but I do not have time to watch TV all night.*

More energy exists now than when dependence was more prevalent. Both are busy advocating their own perceptions and are spending less time trying to understand each other. This interaction intensifies even further when Rob favors unhealthy independence.

Sue: *You watch too much TV!*

Rob: *I do not!*

Sue: *Yes you do!*

Rob: *Look, I work hard and can do anything I want,
so do not lecture me on what I can and can not do!*

The weaknesses of independence become more apparent as we exhibit characteristics of unhealthy independence. When this happens, we are more willing to receive and less likely to give. To be a good partner, we must be willing to give and receive. Unhealthy independent partners have a need for control and can be defensive in an effort to maintain control of their environment. They have great difficulty listening to others' opinions and are quick to blame their problems on others. These individuals are emotionally insecure, but put up a strong emotional front to protect themselves. As you can imagine, these types of behaviors do not foster acceptance, understanding and appreciation.

Interdependence

Dependence-----------Interdependence-----------Independence

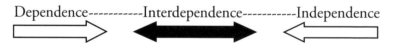

Now that we have identified the attributes of dependence and independence, we can begin to understand how the healthy characteristics of these two opposites combine to form the more stable characteristics of interdependence. Likewise, we can recognize how their unhealthy traits can undermine a relationship, regardless of our intentions.

Interdependence occurs when we embody the strengths of both healthy dependence and healthy independence. This 50/50 balance is not acquired at a particular age. One individual could reach this state of interdependence by seventeen, another by forty-two and still another may never attain it. Achieving interdependence results in assertive, confident individuals, who believe in themselves and, at the same time, are emotionally secure enough to listen, share and understand without feeling intimidated or threatened by the thoughts, feelings and actions of others. By definition, this level of interaction requires a great level of maturity. Do you know of an individual who has reached this level of interdependence? Below is a list of characteristics most common with interdependence.

Characteristics of Interdependence

Willing to listen	Confident
Able to problem solve	Patient
Emotionally secure	Forgiving
Able to make informed decisions	Caring
Mature	Trusting
Willing to take initiative	Willing to take risks
Able to stand up for self	Able to say no
Accepting	Considerate
Dependable	Easy going

What happens when an individual favors interdependence?

If Rob favored interdependence, the discussion with his wife, Sue, would change dramatically.

> Sue: *You watch too much TV!*
>
> Rob: *Why do you think I watch too much TV?*
>
> Sue: *As soon as you get home from work, you turn on the TV and it's on until you go to bed.*
>
> Rob: *When the TV is on, I am not always watching it. What do you find so frustrating?*
>
> Sue: *It seems, whenever I try to talk with you I am in competition with the TV.*
>
> Rob: *So you feel the TV is more important than you or our relationship?*

Sue: *Yes.*

Rob: *Wow! I'm sorry, the TV is not more important than you.*

Sue: *I know, but it feels that way when I cannot get your focused attention.*

Rob: *I understand. I can get totally absorbed in the TV during a show or game.*

Sue: *Yes, you can.*

Rob: *Well, let's see if we can come up with a better balance.*

Sue: *That would be great, thanks.*

As you can see, this interaction went in an entirely different direction than all of the other examples. Rob's goal was first to understand Sue. This was not the case in previous examples. When Rob favored unhealthy dependence he rushed to a solution so as to avoid any tension that might occur between him and Sue. When he favored the unhealthy side of independence, he was offended and pushed Sue away emotionally. Neither of these earlier approaches allowed them to even identify Sue's concern—that the TV was more important than her or the relationship. Hence, the couple never had the opportunity to learn and grow from each other as they did when Rob favored interdependence.

As interdependence grows, problems become recognized as normal occurrences that need to be effectively managed, rather than feared or taken personally. It is important to keep in mind that no individual is perfectly interdependent. This is an ideal state and would be an unrealistic expectation to hold each other to. Instead, we all favor one side of the continuum over the other, although we exhibit a range of characteristics.

Increasing Your Level of Interdependence

Where do you lie on the continuum? Are you more independent or dependent in nature? The ability to understand who you are is as essential to your relationship's long-term success as water is to a tree. Considering everything we have discussed, what side of the continuum do you favor?

Dependence----------Or----------Independence

Whichever side of the continuum you favor now, it is important to keep in mind that your perception of interdependence will change over time. This occurs for many reasons, but perhaps the most influential is that as you age, your level of self-awareness tends to increase. Therefore, it can be both insightful and helpful to ask this question over the years, to see how your self-assessment changes.

Once you identify and accept the side of the continuum you favor, you have a choice. You can either continue as you are or you can intentionally move towards more interdependence. The choice is yours and only yours.

How to move from independence to interdependence

If you favor independence, your opportunity to create more interdependence is in developing more balance by adding healthier dependent traits to your character. This may feel awkward at first, but as you learn to express more healthy dependent behaviors, you begin moving closer to interdependence. As this occurs, your level of emotional maturity builds as well. Contrary to popular opinion, through this process, you do not lose your independence; instead you become more balanced and stronger than ever.

To start creating a little more interdependence in your demeanor, identify several behaviors in which your level of independence overrides your level of dependence. For example, going to the movie you want to see, rather than the one your partner wants to watch.

Identify a handful of situations where you favor
independence.

1. _____
2. _____
3. _____
4. _____
5. _____

Take one of the above behaviors and identify how you can
increase your level of interdependence by being a little more
dependent. For instance, if you typically choose what movie you
would go to, let your partner decide which movie you go to instead.

How will you change one of the independent
behaviors above to increase your level of interdependence?

_____
_____
_____
_____
_____

Committing yourself to following this new expectation
will teach you a lot about yourself. For instance, letting your
partner choose a movie may prove to be stressful at first.
Perhaps your partner takes too long in making a decision or
wants to see a movie that is not the first on your list. When
this occurs, your automatic reaction is to make a decision for
the two of you. Yet, each time you can avoid this natural
desire, you will reinforce a new pattern. In counseling we call
this "stretching your comfort level." Once you have successfully integrated a new behavior, you can start working on
another change. Each time you are successful at making an

additional change, your comfort level increases and makes it easier and easier to create new patterns. Make sure to focus on only one or two behavior changes at a time. Working on too many changes at once will be confusing and often leads to failure.

How to move from dependence to interdependence

If you favor dependence, your opportunity for building more interdependence lies in learning how to become more independent. To accomplish this, you will want to begin expressing and trusting yourself more to build confidence. These changes do not have to be earth-shattering in order to be successful. As a matter of fact, making several small changes will have a lasting impact on your behavior. Identify several behaviors in which your level of dependency overrides your level of independency, such as always letting your partner chose where you go out to eat or what movie you see.

> Identify a handful of situations where you favor dependence.
> 1. _____
> 2. _____
> 3. _____
> 4. _____
> 5. _____

Take a minute and define in more detail how you can change one of the above actions so you are taking a more independent approach. For instance, rather than letting your partner choose where you eat out, you start deciding.

How will you change one of the dependent behaviors above to increase your level of interdependence?

_____

_____

_____

_____

_____

The goal is the same whether you naturally favor the side of independence or dependence. Your objective is to create more interdependence by establishing a new pattern and replacing an old one. Again, when consciously making a change in your behavior, you will know when you are successful. You will simply feel comfortable with the new behavior. Your thoughts and feelings will not be trying to undermine your actions. This transition, however, is not automatic; it takes time and dedication and needs to be something you want. Otherwise, you will revert to what is most comfortable and familiar.

Understanding the Type of Relationship You Have

Now that you understand more about your level of interdependence, what do you know about your partner's level of interdependence? What side of the continuum does he or she favor?

Dependence - - - - - - - - - - - Or - - - - - - - - - - - Independence

Taking into consideration which side of the continuum each of you favors, what is your relationship balance?

❑ Independent / Independent
❑ Dependent / Dependent
❑ Independent / Dependent

So often, we over-focus on the changes our partners need to make in their behavior—in this case, their level of interdependence—rather than focusing on what we can do to help them build their level of interdependence. Avoid this trap by fostering an environment that allows your partner to create more interdependence. This requires a certain level of maturity, awareness and persistence on your part, but it is worth it. If your partner favors independence, it is not always easy to let you make a decision. By understanding this, you can make this transition safer and easier. One way to do this is to talk about this challenge during a neutral time, not when you are in the decision-making process. This will allow you to have a safe healthy discussion in which you can both understand each other. Second, agree on some ground rules, such as—positive reinforcement as soon as you recognize your partner is letting go of some of his/her independence. On the other hand, if your partner favors dependence, you could agree to go along with his/her decision without reprisal. This teaches your partner it is okay (safe) to make a decision in your relationship. Such an approach will create a more supportive environment and allow both partners to build their levels of interdependence.

SUMMARY POINTS

Building your level of interdependence will enhance your relationship by allowing you to give and receive more from each other. The goal is not to favor one side of the continuum over the other, but to achieve a better balance between them. Your best outcomes will come from focusing on your own behavior secondary to your partner's. No matter where you classify your relationship, the opportunity to make positive changes lies in your hands. Seeing the value of interdependence is easy, but following up on it with your actions is not.

Self-Assessment Questions:
- ❏ What side of the continuum do I favor?
- ❏ What side of the continuum does my partner favor?
- ❏ How would I describe the type of relationship we have?
- ❏ How can I create more interdependence in myself?
- ❏ How can I help my partner become more interdependent?

Moving Forward

As you can see, your level of interdependence has a powerful influence on what and how you contribute to your relationship. A defining factor on how much interdependence you can achieve is based on your level of emotional awareness. The next step in *Making Right Turns in Your Relationship* is understanding what emotional awareness is and how to create more in your relationship.

CHAPTER FIVE

Emotional Awareness

"When dealing with people remember
you are not dealing with creatures of logic, but creatures
of emotion, creatures bristling with prejudice
and motivated by pride and vanity."
—Dale Carnegie

The overall effectiveness of your relationship's communication and problem-solving skills will depend on your level of emotional awareness. Your emotions are powerful influences. We have all been in situations which we struggled through with our partner because of the emotional tension that existed between us. In response to situations or events emotions can lead you to get in heated arguments, yell, say things you regret, and slam doors. All of which have a negative impact on your partner, you and your relationship. Because of this, your emotions are critical components to be understood and respected. At the same time, you want to avoid letting them control your behavior and pull your relationship off track. To prevent this from happening, we will review the following concepts to increase your level of emotional awareness and relationship stability.

✓ Understand your emotions
✓ Emotional awareness exercise
✓ Choose to win emotionally

These concepts are not the end-all to building emotional awareness, but in accomplishing each of them, you will significantly enhance your confidence, emotional comfort and level of interdependence. In addition, these improvements will automatically reduce tension and conflict in your relationship and enable you to more effectively communicate and problem solve.

Understand Your Emotions

In isolation, your emotions are as innocent and pure as a child's curiosity. Feelings are not wrong; they are normal attributions of being a person. However, you can respond incorrectly to them. For instance, feeling disappointed when your partner does not buy you flowers on your birthday is one thing, but responding by yelling at or ignoring your partner for a week is another story.

It is important to understand what you are feeling and why you are feeling as you are. Once you understand what and why you are feeling, then you are better able to make healthy choices regarding what you want to do. The inability to understand your feelings and why you are experiencing them will lead you to make unhealthy reactive choices. Therefore, to better understand and respond to your emotions, it is important that you are able to answer the following three questions.

- What am I feeling?
- Why am I feeling?
- What can I do about it?

What am I feeling?

One of the core responsibilities of parenting is teaching children how to connect their experiences to emotions. When a child falls and starts crying, a parent teaches her what she is feeling by identifying where the pain is, how it happened, giving it a kiss, and letting the child know she will be alright. Eventually, the child begins making these connections independently. This training, however, becomes more difficult when it comes to teaching a child how to differentiate between rejection, sadness, disappointment, anger and frustration. Yet, as we transition into adulthood we are not only responsible for knowing how to identify our own emotions, but we are responsible for knowing how to act on them appropriately. As we all know, this is not always an easy task.

The value of recognizing what you are feeling cannot be overstated. For instance, you come home from work, the kitchen is a mess, the phone is ringing, the television is on, the dog is barking, the kids are screaming, your spouse is on her way out the door to a meeting and you're hungry. How do you feel? Are you happy, excited, frustrated, disappointed, angry, indifferent or other? For the sake of this example, let's say you are excited. How would you know this? This question can be answered by understanding "why are you feeling excited?"

Why am I feeling?

As it turns out, the kitchen is a mess because you spent last night making one of your favorite dishes for dinner and went to bed before cleaning up. You are expecting a phone call from your sister in Seattle so you pick up the phone right away, the dog is barking to welcome you home, and the kids are excited to talk with their aunt on the phone. You are planning on cleaning the kitchen and having dinner ready when your spouse returns home. All of these things, some of which you have been looking forward to all day, are exciting.

What can I do about it?

In this case, things are going well, so you really do not

want to change anything. However, when things are not going well, it is important to understand what you can do to change the situation. What if, the kitchen is a mess because the kids did not pick up after themselves, it's a telemarketer on the phone, the dog is barking because the neighbor's dog is in your yard, the kids are fighting over what they want to watch on television, your spouse is going out for the third night this week, and you have no dinner plans? What are you feeling? Why are you feeling? What can you do about it?

At this point, let's say you are frustrated and overwhelmed because you feel like your life is out of control and there is nothing you can do about it. This being the case, you can choose to let these emotions control your behavior or you can take responsibility for the direction your actions take you.

To take control of the situation you could choose to hang up the phone with a quick "thanks, but no thanks," let the dog outside, shut off the television, ask the kids where they want to order pizza from, request that they clean up the kitchen and that they set the table. Later that night you could share your concerns with your partner about not having enough quality time together and begin to problem-solve how you can have more time together.

On the other hand, if you let your feelings control your behavior, you could have responded completely differently. Perhaps you would have turned off the TV, yelled at the kids, opened up your slider door and yelled at your neighbor's dog, eaten leftovers, complained to your spouse, and gone to bed frustrated and with a dirty kitchen to clean up the next day. This reaction to your feelings and emotions will not only drive a large wedge between you and your partner, but it will also prevent you from understanding yourself.

The more effectively you understand what and why you are feeling something, the easier it will be for you to share and choose appropriate behaviors. This level of self-awareness also allows you to recognize potential emotional situations earlier so you can effectively manage them before they get out of control. Without emotional awareness, emotions can flare, frustration grows and things are said and done that no one truly means. As a result, you both end up back-peddling in order to start over. This is a time consuming and exhausting process. One of the easiest ways to gain more emotional self-awareness and to better understand your partner's emotions is to complete the following exercise several times.

Emotional Awareness Exercise

This exercise is intended to help identify and understand your partner's and your own thoughts, feelings and emotions. The challenge of this exercise is to ask each other a series of questions and listen to each other's responses without any rebuttals, judgments or opinions. To complete this emotional awareness exercise, you will need to identify a past emotional event or situation that caused some emotional tension in your relationship and ask each other the following questions.

❑ What were your feelings during the situation?
❑ How did you feel physically?
❑ What other thoughts or emotions did you experience?

The following example should help illustrate the above process. It is based on a past situation in which Peter was an hour late in meeting his wife, Mary, for dinner. By the time he arrived, she had already left. Needless to say, they did not go out to eat or have an enjoyable evening at home.

Past emotional event: *Peter running an hour late for dinner.*

    Mary: *What were your feelings when you were running late?*

81

Peter: *How disappointed you were going to be with
me and I was with myself, especially knowing
that we have not had much time together
over the past few months because of work
and other responsibilities. I wondered just
how upset you were going to be with me and
how I was going make this up to you. I was
thinking you would be expecting a phone call
from me, but because of my rushing around the
office, I left the cell phone on my desk. I also
highly doubted we would have an enjoyable
night together.*

Mary: *How did you feel physically when you were
running late?*

Peter: *My stomach was in a knot. I was breathing
rapidly, my heart pumping, hands sweating
and my thoughts were racing through my
head as I rushed to the restaurant.*

Mary: *What other thoughts or emotions did
you experience?*

Peter: *I was very anxious in anticipation of your
reaction, as well as very frustrated and
disappointed with myself for blowing it again.*

Past emotional event: *Mary waiting for an hour before leaving
the restaurant.*

Peter: *What were your feelings when I was late?*

Mary: *I could not believe you were late, after we had
just talked about it this afternoon. I wondered
if you had gotten caught up in traffic or were in
an accident. I thought about how frequently
you have been late and felt you did not take
seriously the value of our time together. I also*

> *wondered why you had not called so I could know when to expect you.*

Peter: *How did you feel physically during the event?*

Mary: *My face was red; my thoughts were racing much like yours as well as my heart pumping and my fists tense.*

Peter: *What other thoughts or emotions did you experience?*

Mary: *I was embarrassed. The hostess repeatedly asked me if I wanted to sit at a table. I was scared that something might have happened. I was also very angry because you have done this on several occasions. Over all, I felt disrespected and unappreciated.*

What did Mary and Peter learn from this interaction? First, they learned something about themselves. Peter identified his feelings of disappointment, frustration and overall anxiousness. Mary recognized her fear, embarrassment, frustration, and overall feelings that Peter did not respect her. Second, they both identified something about each other. Peter learned that Mary identified his repeated tardiness as apathy towards her, and Mary recognized that Peter actually was upset with himself and cared about her. As a result, Peter became more determined than ever not to be late, and Mary became more patient with Peter because she understood that he really did care.

Going through this process of sharing helped both Peter and Mary clear some emotional tension between them. It also gave them a greater appreciation and respect for each other. Now, if a similar situation occurs in the future, much less negative energy will be consumed. Rather than becoming overwhelmed with frustration, they will be able to slow down, avoid second-guessing each other and discuss the situation.

This will allow them to make better choices and work more closely together, rather than being controlled by emotions that they do not fully understand.

As you attempt this exercise, choose past events that were not too emotionally draining. Choosing too strong an emotional situation to practice with will not enable you to work together. Instead you will get caught up in the old emotional energy, and the value of this exercise will be lost.

It is equally valuable to reflect on your past interactions alone. This is not only insightful, but it will enable you to make changes in your behavior. For instance, upon reflection, you may notice that after a difficult work day you complain about things that are not getting done around the house. You may also realize that this leads to the development of an argument and often, by the end of the night, you are apologizing for your behavior. By going through this exercise by yourself, you can reflect upon and more honestly understand how your emotions have impacted your behaviors. With this insight, you can choose new actions and behaviors to break this old pattern, such as going for a walk with your partner once you get home or ordering out for dinner instead of choosing to cook.

Emotions can lead you aimlessly about without purpose. On their own, they have no direction. By building your level of emotional awareness, you will be able to more clearly understand what and why you are feeling a particular way and can choose to take control of your actions. There is perhaps no better way to do this than by choosing to win emotionally.

Choose to Win Emotionally

Knowing the difference between when you are winning or losing emotionally can provide a tremendous advantage when it comes to choosing your actions. When experiencing a winning state, you feel connected, understood and energized. When caught in a losing state, you feel just the opposite—

disconnected, misunderstood and in opposition with yourself, someone or something. You would not be reading this book if you wanted to lose emotionally. Unfortunately, it is easy to trick yourself into thinking you are winning emotionally when in fact you are losing. The secret is identifying as quickly as possible when you are losing so you can alter your actions and achieve a winning state. To accomplish this we will review the following topics.

- Signs of winning emotionally
- Signs of losing emotionally
- Choosing a direction

Signs of winning emotionally

Think back to a situation in which you were winning emotionally. This may have been as simple as the last time you accomplished a goal, enjoyed an evening out with your spouse, completed a project or laughed hard with friends or family.

Emotional Situation: _____

Once you have identified a situation in which you were winning emotionally, ask yourself the following questions:

❑ How did I feel emotionally?
❑ How did I act?
❑ What did my body feel like?
❑ What did my facial expression look like?
❑ How was I breathing?
❑ What types of thoughts did I have?
❑ How did I treat others?

Make sure you know how you think, feel, respond and act from a physiological, emotional and behavioral position when you are winning. How do you walk, talk, sit, breathe, feel, listen and interact? What are your facial expressions? You want to be able to recognize these components. In doing so, you can learn to more fully appreciate your positive emotional states. This will also help you recognize when you have successfully converted from a losing to a winning state.

When winning emotionally, you feel warm, comfortable, happy and vibrant. Your body feels alive and your thoughts are positive. All in all, you feel healthy in mind, body and spirit. To increase your chances of winning emotionally, set yourself up in situations that will lead to this state. What makes you happy, fulfilled and rewarded? What do you want to accomplish? This could range from spending time with your kids, having great sex, enjoying a hobby, being in shape or going on a vacation. Are you doing at least a few things that increase your happiness? What things have you gotten away from in your relationship? Perhaps in the past you used to enjoy going out to a movie every once in awhile, playing a card or board game, taking a shower together, going for drives in the country or simply sitting down for dinner. Whatever the case, pick up some of your old habits and keep them closer to you so they do not drift away again.

Signs of losing emotionally

Think back to a moment in time in which you were losing. Perhaps you just had a disagreement with your partner, lost something important or had a tough day at work. I am sure you can think of a time in which you were emotionally losing.

Emotional Situation: _____

Once you have identified a situation in which you were

losing emotionally, ask yourself the following questions:

- ❏ How did I feel when losing emotionally?
- ❏ How did I act?
- ❏ What did my body feel like?
- ❏ What did my facial expression look like?
- ❏ How was I breathing?
- ❏ What types of thoughts did I have?
- ❏ How did I treat others?

When losing emotionally, you may feel rushed, your face tense and your blood pressure high. Several years ago I went to an office supply store to make some copies, and Lisa had asked me to pick up some ice cream on my way home. After making copies, I waited about five minutes for the person in front of me to be checked out. At the end of that transaction, the clerk's shift must have ended as she pulled her drawer and walked away, not saying a word. Stunned, I turned around to notice no one else was in the store. I continued to wait anxiously for the next clerk to get arranged. I had a $2.00 order and was getting pretty frustrated. Then, in the middle of my transaction, the clerk was interrupted by a phone call and walked to another part of the store to check something out. Rather than pay for the copies, I was so upset that I walked out. Driving home, not only was I ranting and raving to myself, but also found myself behind a very, very slow driver. There was nowhere to pass, and the ten-minute drive home felt like an eternity. Upon walking in the house, Lisa asked me where the ice cream was. As you can imagine, the rest of the night did not go any better.

It seems once we start losing, we continue losing as it has a "snowball effect." Sometimes a small problem can grow much bigger than it is and ruin a day, weekend or even longer period of time. At what point in this story do you think I started losing? Most people believe I started losing the moment I walked away from the cashier. However, I truly started losing once my thoughts and emotions started to work against me. This occurred when the cashier closed her register. Had I recognized that I was losing emotionally, I could have responded differently. When the clerk started to close the till, I could have asked for my transaction to be finished. Who knows, maybe she had worked two hours over her shift, and if she did not leave right then she would be late for her daughter's basketball game. I could have accepted that. Or, had I realized I was losing, I could have told myself not to worry about it; after all, something as small as this was not a good reason to get my blood pressure up. Contrary to what I thought, I had let the external world control my inner sanctum and I ended up going to bed with a headache.

A few years ago, a friend was backing out of his parking space and nearly hit a car. He was not paying enough attention, and the other car was going too fast in the parking lot. In response to his error, the other driver responded by stopping her car, extending her middle finger and then speeding off, to only park 100 feet away. As he drove by her parked car, she slammed her door and again shared her disapproval with an unfriendly hand gesture. At the time, he thought to himself how unfortunate she was and how lucky he was. Imagine the negative energy and frustration that was passing through her body that could have been better invested. There was a time when his behavior would not have been much different than hers, but he had learned how to win emotionally and chose to do so in this situation.

From time to time we all get a little over-excited, but more often than not, we can choose to win. We just have to recognize that it is a choice. This is one of life's precious secrets to take advantage of. Upon thinking about the concept of emotionally winning or losing, which are you more comfortable with, winning or losing?

Choosing a direction

> *"The longer I live, the more I realize the impact of attitude
> on life. Attitude, to me, is more important than facts. It is
> more important than the past, than education, than money,
> than circumstances, than failures, than successes, than what
> other people think or say or do. It is more important than
> appearance, giftedness, or skill. It will make or break a
> company… a church… a home. The remarkable thing is
> we have a choice every day regarding the attitude we will
> embrace for that day. We cannot change our past…we
> cannot change the inevitable. The only thing we can do is
> play on the one string we have, and that is our attitude.…
> I am convinced that life is 10% what happens to me and
> 90% how I react to it…"*
>
> —*Charles Swindoll*

Life is 10% what happens to you and 90% how you react
to it. The more knowledge and skills you have, the better off
you are. One such skill is learning various distraction techniques to get you back on track before you fall too far off. To
do this, first make sure you understand how you feel physiolog-
ically and psychologically when you are losing. What type of
thoughts run through your mind? How does your body feel?
What type of energy engulfs your body? The better you are at
recognizing these signals, the more quickly you can turn the situation around. The longer it takes you to recognize when you
are losing, the more entwined you will become with your emotions and the less likely you are to get back on track. Whenever
you feel you are losing emotionally, you need to have some skills
to get back on track.

The following are two distraction techniques that are relatively easy to carry out and can provide a more supportive frame of reference rather quickly.

- Taking a time-out
- Breaking the emotional cycle

Taking a time-out

Once you identify you are losing emotionally, stop whatever you are doing and relax. Take a moment and look at things from 10,000 feet rather than being overwhelmed by the moment. Take some deep breaths and slow yourself down. Sometimes, we simply need to pull our emotional car over and turn off the engine. Usually, couples agree that stopping the process is more important than moving forward and making things worse. Therefore, before getting caught in a debate over who said what, stop the verbal jousting and refocus. I know this sounds relatively easy, but we all know that our emotions can get away from us from time to time. When this happens, we tend to take things too seriously, lack flexibility and shut ourselves off to our partner's thoughts and feelings.

A helpful way to initiate the time-out is by establishing a signal, word or phrase that gives you and your partner permission to take a break or start over. I have heard couples use a distracting phrase like "I could go for a piece of chocolate right now" or the word "Spam." It truly does not matter what it is, so long as you both agree on its purpose in advance. Signals can especially be helpful when in public. They allow you to communicate without feeling stressed or having to fully explain yourself. If you think about it, you probably already use non-verbal signals. Perhaps it's the evil eye or the ever-so-common throat clearing. Interestingly enough, the purpose of these signals is often not discussed in advance, leaving much room for error. Again, the goal of a time-out is to stop the negative momentum sooner rather than later. This will provide you the opportunity to refocus and choose the direction your relationship will take.

Breaking the emotional cycle

Every once in a while, both Lisa and I have found ourselves getting uptight with each other due to a combination of many factors. Then one day we learned the value of breaking the emotional cycle. We were camping and had plans to go to a nearby lake the next day. It had rained all night and neither of us slept very well. The following morning, it continued to rain as we packed our tent. We were both frustrated and curt with each other. Unfortunately this only served to create more frustration between us. Once packed, we drove towards the highway to return home rather than go to the lake. Then, for some unknown reason we both recognized that we were losing emotionally. Recognizing this, we decided to get ourselves into a different frame of mind. We rolled down the car windows and screamed at the top of our lungs. Upon doing this, we both immediately felt a release of negative emotional energy, and the tension left our bodies. Although it felt a little funny yelling out the car windows, it caused us to laugh and smile.

With a new frame of reference, we changed our minds and drove to the lake as we had originally planned. Shortly after arriving, the sun broke out and the rest of the day was beautiful. The ironic thing about our change of heart was that it rained all day back at home. Had we not made the change in our emotional state, we are confident that our day would have only become worse.

By breaking the emotional cycle, you get the opportunity to refocus and pull yourself away from the claws of your emotions. Sometimes, a time-out is not enough to get you refocused. It is in these moments that a greater distraction is needed.

Here are several ways to break the emotional cycle with your behavior:

Breaking Your Emotional Cycle

Start dancing or singing
Laugh at yourself
Jump up and down
Roll down the car windows and scream
Hold your hands up in the air while talking
Make funny faces

As a counselor, I have helped many couples break their emotional cycle to get refocused. A common request made was for them to go home and argue. Most found this to be a peculiar request, but there was one catch—they had to argue while holding one hand in the air. Almost always, as a result of this cycle breaker, couples reported that they ended up laughing at each other and could not argue. This de-escalated their emotions and allowed them to start listening to each other. Distraction techniques are really helpful at providing you an emotional break. Whichever methods you choose, make sure to discuss them with your partner in advance. By agreeing to yell at the top of your lungs together, you are working as a team. In doing this you are not only building a bond with your partner, but you are increasing the chances that this distraction technique will work.

The goal of distraction techniques is not to avoid your feelings and emotions; rather, it is to embrace them and choose a healthy direction. Through practice and time, these two approaches, taking a time-out and breaking the emotional cycle, can become useful techniques for keeping you on track in your relationship. Remember, life does not lead you; you lead your life.

SUMMARY POINTS

Understanding and accepting the complexity of your emotional being can lead to developing an internal locus of control, rather than being controlled by external events, people and situations. Emotions are not wrong, but if you let them lead your actions, you will be guided aimlessly about. Instead, your goals should lead your actions, not your emotions. Through practice, you will enhance your personal awareness and learn to understand and share your feelings. In addition, by choosing to win emotionally, you choose a positive direction for your thoughts, feelings and behaviors. This allows you to recognize when you or your relationship is losing emotionally, and gives you a chance to get back on track.

Self-Assessment Questions:
- ❑ How would I rate my level of emotional awareness?
- ❑ How good am I at understanding my partner's feelings and emotions?
- ❑ How do I react with my emotions and feelings?
- ❑ How do I take the time to understand my own feelings before I act?
- ❑ How do I take the time to understand my partner's feelings?
- ❑ How have I chosen to win emotionally?
- ❑ How do I break negative emotional cycles so my relationship can win?

Moving Forward

Clearly, by improving your level of emotional awareness, you will create more right turns in your relationship. To further enhance your relationship, the next chapter will help you understand the rules you live by and how they influence your thoughts, feelings and actions.

Making Right Turns in Your Relationship

CHAPTER SIX

The Rules You Live By

"Nothing is so firmly believed
as that which we least know."
–Michel de Montaigne

There are two certainties we have all learned to expect as fundamental components to life. These are death and taxes. For the purpose of this chapter, I would like to include an additional item to this list—rules. What are rules? Rules represent the standards – the beliefs and values – by which we live. Rules are the fabric of our lives.

Everywhere you go and everything you do is defined by some set of rules. Your relationship rules may be imposed by your partner or you. These can vary from how fast you can drive, how to eat, how to save money, how to communicate or how to fold the laundry. Each rule sets an expectation or standard to follow, and we all have established a unique set of rules in our lives.

In any relationship, healthy or not, there are differences in rules that are certain to collide. This is an unavoidable reality that we all face. For instance, Lisa and I have different rules about cleaning. She believes the house is not clean until every last speck and particle has been wiped down. As a result, cleaning the house is a major project. I, on the other hand, believe the house is good to go when there are no piles that need picking up. These different rules cause tension from time to time. Due to Lisa's rules, she will let piles accumulate; after all, she plans on cleaning everything up over the weekend. I find these piles distracting and frustrating, so I complain as I am picking them up. Yet, when I clean things, I am not as detailed as she is. As you can imagine, she finds this bothersome and cleans areas again that I have already done. When this happens, I become less interested in cleaning; after all, she is going to do it over anyway. We both simply have different sets of rules about cleaning that cause turmoil in our interactions. What about your relationship? Can you think of differences in your rules that cause conflict?

Differences are normal and to be expected. Therefore, there is no reason for them to become sore spots in our relationships. However, it is important that we learn how to manage these differences effectively. There is a myth that couples with the most compatibility have the greatest likelihood of success. This is not always the case; compatibility only suggests less dissimilarity to manage. Even the most compatible couples have differences. Therefore, their ultimate success will be determined by how well they work through and grow from their different rules.

We all know couples who were highly compatible, but whose relationships failed. Likewise, we also know couples who did not appear very compatible, but whose relationships matured very well through the years because they effectively managed their rules. *It is not your compatibility, it is your ability to identify, understand and adjust to each other's rules that will make or break your relationship.*

We all carry a few unhealthy, false or limiting rules at our side. Even more importantly, we have many more healthy and helpful rules. By accepting your rules not as absolutes, but as <u>choices</u>, you will be better able to compromise and accommodate one another.

Recognizing your rules as choices provides you with a filter to make decisions based on your future goals rather than on your past experiences. When you have differences in your rules (such as how to clean the house), it is important that both of you can recognize your perspective as a choice rather than an absolute. If Lisa and I both felt that the other's cleaning methodology was inherently wrong, we would establish a long-standing conflict in our relationship. This choice would create a barrier and consume unnecessary emotional energy. As a result, we would both lose because of our inability to compromise and problem-solve together.

To better understand your rules and how to manage them, we will review the following.

- ✓ How do rules develop?
- ✓ Why do you need rules?
- ✓ Why do you impose your rules on your partner?
- ✓ How to take control of your rules
- ✓ What happens when a rule is broken?
- ✓ How to manage your rules through greater interdependence
- ✓ Which type of rule does your relationship struggle with the most?

How do Rules Develop?

Your rules began developing long before you were even aware they existed. The person you are today is a reflection of everything that has happened to you and your responses to those experiences. To some extent this process is automatic and unconscious. Each and every one of your experiences has built upon one another to establish the complicated set of rules you live by today. The result is an internal network far more complicated than any computer. Rather than being designed by silicon chips, your rules are established by the neurological network of your nervous system and brain.

Eventually, after a number of years, your rules turn into patterns. These patterns form the foundation from which you grow and by which you live. If you did not trust people as a teenager, it is likely that this pattern will carry into your adulthood. Of course, the opposite is also true. If you trusted people when you were younger, chances are you still do today. Does this mean your infancy, childhood and adolescent years are the sole determinant of who you will be as an adult? Not entirely! As you can imagine, little thought went into developing your rules as a child, adolescent, or even a young adult. By investigating different perspectives, your awareness can be broadened, new rules acquired and behaviors formed.

A vast majority of your rules developed unconsciously in reaction to emotions, past experiences and expectations. This is why you are so comfortable with and believe in them. They developed side by side with your physical development. They are as natural to you as the beating of your heart. This is what makes them so hard to understand fully. But, like much else in your life, your rules are a choice!

There is a false assumption that "if you have a belief it must be right." I remember hearing a story about how a granddaughter learned the secret of her grandmother's fine turkey dinner. One year at Thanksgiving the little girl asked her mom why she cut the turkey in half before cooking it. The mother explained that this was a long-standing secret she learned from watching her own mother cook the family turkey. At the dinner table the little girl could not resist asking her grandmother if she too had learned this secret from her mother. The grandmother replied, "Heavens no! The only reason I cut our turkey in half was because the oven was not big enough to hold it whole." This story illustrates that things are not always as they seem. We should question our own rules from time to time to check their validity. There is no need to accept old rules if they are blocking you from reaching your goals. You can continue developing, expanding and maturing your rules throughout your life. Are your rules supporting your relationship goals?

Why do You Need Rules?

You need and depend on rules to provide structure, familiarity, predictability and stability to your everyday life. Like it or not, we are all creatures of habit and trust our rules to get us through both the good and the bad. When in a disagreement, what do you do? Do you ignore the conflict? Do you discuss each other's needs, wants and expectations? Do you respond with anger? Do you resolve your disagreement only after getting frustrated and blowing up at each other? Whatever the case, you depend on a set of rules to get you through the situation.

The benefit of your rules is that they help guide your decisions and behaviors. In many cases this saves time and energy. For example, you do not need to learn how to remake the bed everyday or how to take a shower. However, there are two dangers that come along with the benefit of structure. First, some older rules may no longer be supporting your relationship goals. A husband believing that he should never have to buy his wife flowers or a wife feeling that the best way to get her point across is by yelling are examples of existing rules that are doing more harm than good. Second, we can become so dependent on our rules that they can limit our flexibility and adaptability. A husband stuck on not buying flowers, to prove a point, is going to miss many genuine opportunities demonstrate his affection. A wife determined to yell to get her point across will undermine the emotional intimacy she so deeply seeks.

Managing a balance between the familiarity and predictability of your rules with the need to be flexible and adaptive is one of the single greatest struggles we all face. Life brings with it many experiences, and they cannot all be treated alike. By using your rules as a sounding board, you are better able to bring flexibility to your life and respond to the challenges and opportunities that present themselves.

Why do You Impose Your Rules on Your Partner?

It is both a natural and fundamental instinct to impose your perception of truth (rules) on those around you, especially your partner. There are two reasons for doing this. First, it supports and reinforces the belief system you have learned to trust and respect. The second reason we impose our rules is, more often than not, we want to help those around us. After all, what's true for us must be helpful for others, right?

Your body provides you a physical presence, but your rules provide you the mental and emotional substance. Like everyone else, you are reluctant to toss aside what you have learned to expect and trust. Your rules have provided you great comfort and stability by helping define who you are, what you believe in and what you do. Therefore, when the first time your partner made the bed or sorted the laundry differently than you do, you had a reaction. Perhaps you showed him a better way to make the bed; since you like the sheets on the bed tucked and your partner does not tuck them.

Have you ever known your partner was right about something, but because it went against what you had always done, you were resistant anyway? This is a sure sign of just how intrinsic and powerful your rules can become. The less you understand your rules, the more you will defend them. The more understanding you have of your rules, the less pressure you feel to impose them and the more appreciative you will be of other's rules. Understanding that there is more than one way to cook a turkey may be confusing and risky, but in trying different recipes you may find a new one that is so good that it is hard to believe you ever cooked it differently.

How to Take Control of Your Rules

"I know of no more encouraging fact than the unquestionable ability of man to elevate his life by a conscious endeavor."
—*Henry David Thoreau*

Your rules come together and represent your similarities, differences and the uniqueness of your relationship. When you think of improving your relationship, there is no better means than taking control of your rules. It is very common for couples to disagree and argue over items that are not worth their energy. Yet, at the same time, they avoid discussing items that a mutual decision is of utmost importance. To take control of your rules, you will want to differentiate between three categories of rules.

- Preferences
- Negotiables
- Boundaries

In total, these three categories encompass all of your relationship's rules. Each has unique characteristics and properties as well as solutions for managing them. Classifying your relationship problems into one of these three categories not only allows you to identify what type of challenge you are dealing with, but gives you possible solutions for managing them. Identifying and knowing how to respond allows you to stay focused while facing a variety of challenges. As a result, you will be less interested in imposing your rules and more interested in listening to your partner and moving towards solutions, resolutions and agreements.

As a rule of thumb, you have more preferences than negotiables and more negotiables than boundaries.

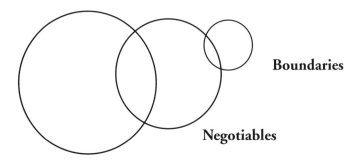

Boundaries

Negotiables

Preferences

You will notice that preferences overlap negotiables and
negotiables overlap boundaries. I would certainly agree that
managing your rules would be easier if no overlapping existed,
but this unfortunately is not the case. As we move from one
category to another, we find some carry-over between them.
In these gray areas, it can become particularly difficult to differentiate between a preference and a negotiable or a negotiable and a boundary. When crossing this type of intersec-
tion, you are going to need to make a decision on what you
are going to call it. It is important to keep in mind that
whether you identify it as a preference, negotiable or boundary is not nearly as important as agreeing on the decision.

Reaching a healthy balance between preferences, negotiables and boundaries is a lifetime adventure. It requires
understanding the differences between them and knowing
where your strengths and weaknesses are with each category,
so that you can continually improve upon them.

To help you in this effort, we will review preferences,
negotiables and boundaries in detail. We will also review how
each of them can be effectively managed to improve upon the
quality of your relationship.

Preferences

Preferences are your least demanding or critical set of rules to be concerned about. However, they do account for a majority of your rules, and if not well-managed, they can undermine your relationship one small step at a time. Preferences represent the "little differences" between your rules and are insignificant to your overall physical or emotional well-being. Here are a few examples of preferences:

Preferences
Whether you rinse out cans and bottles
Which way the toilet paper rolls off the roll
How to squeeze the toothpaste
Where to hang the towels
How to do dishes, laundry or iron
How you like your meat cooked
How to boil pasta
Where you hang a picture

How you squeeze the toothpaste has little impact on the quality of your life. However, if allowed to come between your partner and you, this insignificant rule can consume a great deal of unnecessary energy. At a presentation I was giving several years ago, a gentlemen came up to me and said, "I know this sounds silly, but what finally broke my marriage was how my wife squeezed the toothpaste tube." He went on to explain that she would squeeze it from the middle and did not put the top back on. Certainly, the toothpaste was not the source of this relationship's problem, but it was plain to see that they were not managing their preferences. It is not necessarily the large problems that eat away at an otherwise healthy relationship; often it is the build-up of many small disagreements that do.

Managing your preferences

We all accommodate and compromise on many preferences in our relationships. Often, this is done without even knowing it—for example, putting on a sweatshirt rather than turning up the heat when your partner is comfortable and you are cold. At other times, the compromise is more intentional—for example, a wife choosing to support her husband's need to start a home recycling program even though it is not important to her.

Can you think of any preferences that you have become accustomed to and have accepted in your relationship? Imagine if you had chosen not to let go of or compromise on any of these items. Instead of feeling comfortable, you would be harboring many negative thoughts and feelings towards each other. This would have only added unnecessary strain to the normal challenges your relationship will face. Fortunately, we all have enough challenges in our relationships without adding the unnecessary stress of arguing over preferences.

I can think of two preferences that once created tension between Lisa and me. She always locked the dead bolt whenever she left the house. This was frustrating to me; I did not like unlocking both the regular lock and the dead bolt, especially when carrying something. Another preference that created problems was where the cutting board should be stored in the kitchen. We both had different preferences. She liked it next to the stove and I preferred it next to the refrigerator. Yes, I know, these examples seem petty, but that is what makes them preferences.

It is very easy to make more out of a situation than necessary, especially when it comes to preferences. Some rules are important to discuss while others are not; the secret is recognizing the difference. For us, acknowledging both the cutting board and dead bolt as nothing more than preferences, was a relief. It allowed us, for the first time, to sit back and recognize what battles we should and should not choose in our relationship. This may not sound like much, but because of it, we chose to let these preferences go. As a result, we have two fewer variables tugging at our relationship. Interestingly enough, today the cutting board is neither next to the stove or next to the refrigerator; instead, it is in a lower kitchen cabinet.

The solution to managing your preferences is simply letting go of some of your own rules (such as how the lawn has to be mowed) and accepting some of your partner's preferences (such as how to fold the laundry). It is this acceptance that allows you to enjoy life and each other more. Take a moment to identify a few preferences that are creating negative energy and stress in your relationship.

Preferences that are creating negative energy and stress.
1. _____
2. _____
3. _____
4. _____
5. _____

Choose one preference from your list that you are willing to accommodate or let go of. Stating that you will let go of this preference is easier said than done. Your desire to make this change has to be a genuine commitment to yourself. If the value of letting go is not recognized, then your commitment will be a fading gesture. Think about the benefits of letting go of this preference and the consequences of holding on to it. Once you are committed to letting go, it takes a little time for the change to settle in, but remember your feelings will follow your actions. Eventually, the new behavior will feel comfortable at all levels—emotionally, cognitively and physically. Lisa and I knew that we reached this state when neither the cutting board nor dead bolt caused any negative thoughts, feelings or apprehension. Once you have achieved this state you are ready to take on another preference.

Celebrate your successes! Each time you integrate a preference, you have made your life less stressful and demanding. Recognize these accomplishments. Be proud of what you have accomplished. Buy yourself a small gift, go out to dinner—whatever you do, celebrate. Similarly, if you notice your partner being more tolerant of a preference acknowledge it with appreciation. Don't miss this opportunity. Too often we wait for everything to be perfect before we provide positive feedback. This approach is backwards. We should always be looking for opportunities to praise our partners. This teaches them to repeat the wanted behaviors.

The goal of managing your preferences is to let go of as many as possible. By letting go of just four preferences a year, just one every three months, you would in combination let go of eight distractions in your relationship. What a gift to give yourselves. Over the course of a few years, almost all of your preferences will be effectively managed. Any way you slice it, not spending time arguing over preferences will decrease negative energy and enhance cooperation and respect. I am not suggesting your relationship will be perfect as a result of this one action, but it can be substantially improved by taking charge of your preferences, rather than letting them take control of you. Life is far too short to spend fussing over the little things.

Negotiables

Negotiables are those rules that lie between the flexibility of preferences and the rigidity of boundaries. By choosing to manage your negotiables successfully, you are clearly at an advantage. Examples of negotiables:

Negotiables

How to save money for retirement
Which house to buy
Where to go on vacation
What type of car to purchase
How to discipline your children
What the expectations are for watching TV and bedtime
What school your children will attend
How to manage your debt
How to manage the holidays
What your religious affiliation and practices will be
What tone of voice you can talk to each other in
How often you can go out with your friends
What type of sexual intimacy you will share

You can see from these examples that negotiables are part of your everyday activity and learning how to manage them has a defining impact on your relationship. However, if you are having difficulty managing your preferences, it will be more difficult to manage negotiables. There is a fine line between where a preference ends and a negotiable begins, but understanding that there is a difference allows you to prioritize where you should invest your time and energy and where you should not.

Managing your negotiables

Sometimes negotiables are very easy to manage and other times they are not. It all depends on how similar your needs and expectations are. When needs and expectations are in agreement, negotiable topics are relatively easy to manage. Hence, no extraordinary skills nor extra energy are required. A good example would be a couple who wants to go on a vacation to Paris and who both want to spend most of their time seeing all the sights and sounds of the town.

It is only when differences arise that skills are needed to resolve negotiables. Perhaps a couple agrees they want to go to Paris, but one wants to see all the historic sites, and the other wants to spend their time eating authentic meals and drinking French wine. Coming to an agreement in this case will take additional listening skills, compromising and accommodating.

We are all faced with a multitude of negotiables that will need to be managed in our relationships. It may come as no surprise that a majority of couples face similar negotiable items: such as how to save money, live a satisfactory lifestyle, enjoy their sex life, be happy, manage work, raise children, care for elderly parents and maintain their own health. Even though we are faced with many of the same negotiables, every couple's solutions are a little different than the next. In later chapters we will discuss how to better manage negotiables through communication, understanding, problem-solving and creating change.

Boundaries

The opposite of your preferences are boundaries. Boundaries represent a minority of your rules, and their purpose is to establish clear limits and expectations. They preserve the physical and emotional boundaries of the relationship and self. Just as society creates rules to maintain civil order, your relationship system requires guiding principles to keep it focused and secure. The following are examples of potential boundaries:

Boundaries

No physical abuse
No verbal abuse
No drinking and driving
No sexual acts without mutual consent
No drugs allowed
No extramarital affairs accepted
No letting the kids get between partners
No hitting the children
No going out with friends several nights a week
Maintain personal issues within the relationship

It is not uncommon for preferences and negotiables to be treated like boundaries. More than one spouse has wanted to enforce the proper technique for folding laundry as a boundary. Still others want to indoctrinate their parenting skills as the only option in the household. What makes a boundary unique from a preference or negotiable is that it is non-negotiable. A boundary's very existence is to establish clear expectations and limits for both of you to follow. Making boundaries negotiable would contradict their purpose.

Managing your boundaries

First and foremost, your personal and relationship boundaries should be something discussed, defined and understood. Far too often, just the opposite occurs; these rules are left to assumptions, each partner believing the other should simply know what behaviors are and are not acceptable. Assuming there is an agreed-upon boundary is risky. Nothing will get you in trouble faster than this false assumption. Do not take this risk; avoid mind-reading when it comes to boundaries. What is true for you is not automatically true for your partner. The lines of the relationship need to be drawn up front. Doing so makes it unmistakably clear what is and is not acceptable behavior in the relationship.

A fundamental component of creating your relationship boundaries is knowing what is important to you. Take a minute to identify the items that represent your personal boundaries.

What are your personal boundaries?
1. _____
2. _____
3. _____
4. _____
5. _____
6. _____

Once you have completed the above list, share it with your partner. Likewise, have your partner share his/her personal boundaries. Discussing and establishing these boundaries are important. From your combined list identify your relationship boundaries.

What are your relationship boundaries?
1. _____
2. _____
3. _____
4. _____
5. _____
6. _____

It is important that each of the above boundaries are discussed and understood. Both you and your partner will need to be committed to them, as each is a non-negotiable.

Unfortunately, as I pointed out earlier, there are times where negotiables and boundaries overlap between partners. For instance, one partner may feel that raising voices at each other is a negotiable and the other may see it as a boundary. Discussing these differences will allow partners to understand each other's definition and may lead to a clearer understanding. For example, upon discussion a couple decides that raising one's voice in private is okay, but doing so in a public setting would be disrespectful and unacceptable. Working through these gray areas can prove difficult. However, at no time should you break a personal or relationship boundary unless you reach a new mutual-agreement beforehand.

What Happens When a Rule is Broken?

A broken rule could either be a mutually-agreed-upon negotiable or an established boundary. In either event, you will be faced with the obstacle of rebuilding the trust and respect that has been lost. For example, if your partner has an affair, you will experience a host of emotions: anger, sadness, jealousy, hate, disgust, pity, embarrassment, inadequacy, and many others. Working through these various emotional pains takes a great amount of commitment, time, emotional energy and teamwork. Unfortunately, these different emotions can lead to many alternative responses. Some individuals choose to end their relationship because of the emotional damage that has occurred. Others are able to resolve their long-standing problems that led to the situation in the first place. Still others choose to avoid the problem, fall into depression or get even by having their own affair.

Certainly, the best way to avoid these challenges is to adhere to your established relationship rules. However, when an agreed-upon rule has been broken, there are three steps that will help your relationship rebuild.

- Enforce a consequence
- Accept responsibility
- Choose forgiveness

Enforce a consequence

The first step to getting your relationship back on track is enforcing a consequence. This can be accomplished by the following three actions.

1. Identify in no uncertain terms what rule has been broken and re-establish it as a fundamental principle in your relationship.
2. Share your disappointment in your partner's actions. Focus on the action and the emotional discomfort it has brought to you and the relationship.
3. Enforce a consequence. When an agreed-upon rule has been broken, it can not be treated casually. Instead, a clear message needs to be made that there has been a violation at the relationship's core.

One of the goals of establishing a consequence is to stop the agreed-upon rule from being broken again. When a rule is broken and no consequence follows, you have given permission for it to be broken again. Parents set expectations for their kids around curfew times, and if no consequence follows when the rule is broken, no accountability is established. As a result, the child will continue to break this rule. The same is true in a relationship. If a spouse is allowed to break a boundary and have an affair, what is going to stop him/her from doing it again? It is your responsibility to impose a consequence and preserve your relationship rules. The imposed consequence is best served swiftly, the closer to the incident the better. Therefore, when your partner breaks the rule, you should not wait until the next week to discuss it. Your partner needs to be held accountable immediately.

Exactly what a consequence should be for breaking an agreed-upon rule varies from couple to couple. For instance, take into consideration the following situation. A husband stays out all night with friends without calling his wife to let her know what was happening. This situation will be treated differently by different partners. In one marriage, the wife may request that her husband does not go out with friends again over the next three months. In another marriage, the wife may have a very stern conversation about the behavior, making sure not only to share her disappointment, but also making it absolutely clear that his behavior was unacceptable. In still another marriage, the wife may require he sleeps on the couch for a few days. In any of these cases, the consequences are intended to prevent the behavior from ever happening again. The more severe the broken rule, the more severe the consequence should be. Therefore, the consequence for breaking a boundary is greater than it would be for breaking a negotiable.

When an agreed-upon negotiable or boundary has been broken, and while it is being "repaired," avoid making any major decisions. Emotions can run rampant after your partner has broken an established rule. I have seen spouses filled with immense frustration go out and buy an expensive item in order to bring some happiness into their lives. Unfortunately, this action can bring additional tension to the situation and make it more difficult to resolve. Before any major decisions are made, the broken rule needs to be addressed and discussed by the couple so a plan of action can be defined.

Accept responsibility

The second step to rebuilding your relationship is accepting the consequences for one's actions. Breaking an agreed-upon negotiable or an established boundary cannot be fully cured with a genuine "I'm sorry." Re-establishing trust and respect is simply not as easy as replacing a broken dish. You have emotionally scarred your relationship, and like any other wound, it must be nurtured and cared for before it is healed. It is important to remember that it does not matter if you intended to break a rule or not. You will still need to take responsibility by completing the following tasks.

➤ Accept responsibility without excuses
➤ Accept the consequence imposed by your partner
➤ Take ownership for the solution
➤ Ask for forgiveness
➤ Never break the rule again

If you did not call your partner to discuss what time you were going to get home, you're going to have to accept responsibility for your actions. You cannot blame it on too many drinks or a dead cell phone battery. You will need to apologize and let your partner know you are sorry for your behavior and the discomfort that it has caused. You will need to ask for forgiveness, promise not to break the rule again and follow through with that promise. These actions allow you to take ownership for the solution.

Unfortunately, if you are unwilling to accept responsibility for your actions or blame them on others, then problems are only going to build further, and eventually the relationship will fail. I firmly believe that relationships do not just fail; it takes a lot of hard work and consistency to drive a stake between two people who once cared for each other.

Choose forgiveness

> *"The weak can never forgive.*
> *Forgiveness is the attribute of the strong."*
> —*Mahatma Gandhi*

One of the greatest emotional challenges in your relationship is choosing to forgive. What makes forgiveness so difficult is that in many cases, it is a choice before a feeling. That is, you may not feel 100% comfortable just because you have forgiven your partner. However, when an established boundary or agreed-upon negotiable has been broken, the relationship will not be able to move forward successfully until you choose to forgive. Of course, your partner's willingness to take responsibility and accept the consequences for his or her behavior is also essential to helping your relationship move forward.

We all must learn how to forgive. If you do not, both your personal happiness and your relationship's happiness will be limited by the contempt held in your heart. Forgiveness is something you must be willing to choose. You have to take a chance and forgive even at the risk of being emotionally injured again. Of course, the opposite is also true; you will need to be forgiven at one time or another. If you need to be forgiven, make sure you create a safe environment for your partner. You will need to rebuild your partner's trust and respect with your words and actions.

If you find yourself getting closer to breaking an established boundary or agreed-upon negotiable, stop whatever you are doing. When things are not going well, adding fuel to the fire is not a solution. If something is going astray, find out what it is. It is better to solve your current problem than to create a larger, more difficult one.

If your partner repeatedly breaks a boundary or an agreed-upon negotiable, you will be faced with making a choice, and unfortunately forgiveness is not always the appropriate answer. You cannot continue to put your physical and emotional well-being aside. You will need to stand up for yourself and be willing to walk away from your relationship. Counseling is strongly advised in this situation.

How to Manage Your Rules
Through Greater Interdependence

By this time, you should clearly understand the difference between preferences, negotiables and boundaries. You should also have a good idea of which one of these you struggle with the most. Once acquired, this knowledge will help you better understand and manage your rules. One of the easiest ways of doing this is by increasing your level of interdependence.

If you are more independent than dependent, you will establish more negotiables and boundaries than necessary and fewer preferences. This makes you less flexible and more rigid in your application of rules. Therefore, you have greater difficulty managing preferences. How the toilet paper rolls, which way you fold the towels and how to use the grill are all significant details. You have logical expectations for how each of these is done and when not performed to your standards (rules), you find it distracting. For example, you prefer to heat up the grill to full temperature before cooking and keep the top closed while grilling; whereas your partner turns on the grill, throws on the hamburgers and leaves the top open. Because of your rule, you will find this method of grilling distracting.

Similarly, you treat many of your negotiables as if they were boundaries. For instance, you become very upset whenever your partner does not adhere to some approved plan like bedtime for the kids. When this happens you may get upset and yell or get quiet and walk away.

To better manage your rules and become more interdependent, create more preferences in your life and reduce the number of negotiables and boundaries. Of course, the biggest challenge you will have in accomplishing these tasks will be the loss of control you will feel. A big part of you will want to maintain the false sense of control your negotiables and boundaries have been providing you.

If you are more dependent than independent, you will establish more preferences than necessary and fewer negotiables and boundaries. As a result, you will face fewer conflicts and problems in your relationship. You may see your openness and flexibility as a strength, but your own needs, wants, expectations and feelings will be overlooked from time to time. You will also too quickly accept apologies when boundaries are broken and avoid enforcing consequences.

To better manage your rules and become more interdependent, create fewer preferences in your life and increase the number of negotiables and boundaries. Of course, the biggest challenge you will have in accomplishing these tasks will be overcoming the guilt you will feel from taking more control over what you want, think or feel. This will be uncomfortable, but it is a necessary step towards interdependence.

If you are more interdependent in nature, you will have an easier time identifying your rules into the right category. Boundaries will be clear and forthright, preferences will not be allowed to grow between you, and negotiables will be treated with a focus on collaboration. Therefore, your goal will be in continually observing your behavior and making sure to maintain your interdependence.

Which Type of Rule Does Your Relationship Struggle With the Most?

All relationships can benefit from improving their management of preferences, boundaries and negotiables. However, this task can be confusing. To make it more manageable you need to identify which type of rule your relationship struggles with the most and make it the focus of improvement. Complete the following exercise so you can identify which type of rule you and your partner need to work on together in order to strengthen your relationship.

1. Identify challenges that seem to come up over and over in your relationship.
2. Classify each of these challenges as either a preference, negotiable or boundary.

Ongoing challenges in your relationship

	P	N	B
1._____	( )	( )	( )
2._____	( )	( )	( )
3._____	( )	( )	( )
4._____	( )	( )	( )
5._____	( )	( )	( )
6._____	( )	( )	( )
7._____	( )	( )	( )
8._____	( )	( )	( )
9._____	( )	( )	( )
10._____	( )	( )	( )
Total	___	___	___

Once you identify each of these challenges as either a preference, negotiable or boundary, a pattern should emerge. Through this exercise, Lisa and I learned that most of our relationship challenges did not have anything to do with boundaries. Instead, we let too many of our preferences turn into negotiables. We simply let the little things in life get between us and needed to let go of our minor differences. Learning to treat preferences as preferences and not as negotiables has saved us a tremendous amount of time and energy.

Whether preferences, negotiables or boundaries are making your relationship more challenging, there is something you can do about it. Awareness is the first key to success, but practice, of course, will be the ultimate source of your success. If your relationship struggles with preferences, you are going to have to help each other let go of some of the little things. If you struggle with boundaries or negotiables your emotional awareness, communication and problem solving skills are going to be essential to your success.

> *"If you always do*
> *What you've always done*
> *You'll always get*
> *What you've always got"*
> —*Author Unknown*

SUMMARY POINTS

Your rules are choices. It is by challenging and understanding your rules that you can begin to make more conscious decisions. If your rules are not choices, then you are controlled by them. Do not let this happen to you or your relationship. Make sure you choose the rules you live by and that they support your relationship vision.

Improve your relationship by understanding the type of rules that challenge it. The next time you are having a disagreement, identify which type of rule you are discussing. Is it a boundary, negotiable or a preference? Then you can act accordingly. If it is a preference, let it go; if it is a boundary or negotiable, it will be your level of emotional awareness along with your communication and problem-solving skills that will allow you to effectively manage it.

Self-Assessment Questions:
  ❑ How do I make my rules choices?
  ❑ How have I chosen to manage my preferences?
  ❑ How well have I learned to manage negotiables?
  ❑ How have we established mutual boundaries?
  ❑ How do I respect boundaries?

❑ Which type of rule will I benefit the most by improving: preferences, negotiables or boundaries?
❑ Which type of rule is my relationship most challenged by: preferences, negotiables or boundaries?

Moving Forward

Now that we have discussed the influence of our rules, it's time to focus on building healthy communication skills. In the next chapter, we will define the basic skills of communication. Learning and applying healthy communication skills will allow you to manage your preferences, negotiables and boundaries even more effectively. As you can imagine, this will further enable you to make more right turns in your relationship and life.

CHAPTER SEVEN

Communication

*"I have never in my life learned anything
from any man who agreed with me."*
—Dudley Field Malone

We are all familiar with the term "communication." It is one of the most stated causes for either a successful or unsuccessful relationship. When our communication is effective, it allows us to problem-solve, make decisions, and work together, regardless of whether we are discussing preferences, negotiables or boundaries. Unfortunately, we can get caught up in our emotions and a host of other variables during communication. This causes us to lose track of our overall goal. As a result, we find ourselves in deeper conflict without a clear way out. The purpose of this chapter is to provide a clear understanding of what healthy communication is and how to achieve it.

What is Communication?

Communication is the process of sending, receiving and interpreting information. In your relationship, effective communication occurs when the interpretation of a message you received matches that which your partner intended. The intent of this message could be either positive or negative. If your intended message was to share disappointment, and this is the message your partner received, then effective communication occurred. Ineffective communication, on the other hand, takes place when the interpreted message does not match that which was intended. In this case, if your intended message was to share disappointment, and your partner interpreted it as anger, then effective communication has not occurred. When there is a breakdown in communication, mixed messages and misunderstandings occur between the sender and receiver. This can be confusing and frustrating especially when you have something important to share.

When we think of the importance of communication, we often think of it in "healthy terms." That is, our overall communication is moving us in the direction of our relationship goal. Unfortunately, it is hard to achieve healthy communication if you perceive conflict, disagreements and tension as signs of ineffective communication only. Communication, especially with your intimate partner, is not perfect. Healthy communication is a process, not an event, and sometimes in this process things can become tense, emotions flair and disagreements occur. Often, this static is an important part of reaching an understanding. We are not computers; we have feelings, needs, expectations, past experiences and future expectations filtering much of what we send, interpret and understand. Because of this, in an effort to understand and make decisions, we often take steps backwards before making progress forward.

The messages we send and receive are further complicated by the differences in our rules. For instance, you could agree, the night before, to leave for vacation at 9:00 a.m. on Saturday morning. However, for you this could mean at 9:00 a.m. you will be on the road, and for your partner it could mean being mostly ready by 9:00 a.m. and on the road by 9:30 a.m. So, even when you think you understand each other, it is not always the case. Your communication will not be perfect. Expecting a perfect process of sending and receiving information without any mixed messages or misunderstandings is unrealistic. The purpose of healthy communication is not to eliminate tension, but instead to move productively through it in an effective manner.

The Tools of Communication

Communication is constant. It has no beginning or end. Whether you are sleeping, walking, exercising or talking you are communicating something. Your posture, attitude and general demeanor all speak volumes. This means in order to communicate effectively you will need to take ownership for the messages you send and receive. Four of your most powerful communication tools for doing this are:

✓ Body language
✓ Tone of voice
✓ Words
✓ Congruency

In previous chapters we have discussed many different topics that influence your relationship's success, such as winning emotionally, creating greater interdependence, focusing on the positive and making your relationship a priority. All of these actions send messages and build patterns in your relationship. Likewise, your body language, tone of voice, words and level of congruency can either enhance or undermine the effectiveness of these messages. Understanding the difference between these communication tools and learning how to use them to your advantage can significantly enhance your relationship.

Body Language

When asked which of these four communication tools is the most important, the common belief is that it is our words.

This seems rightfully so, but it is not the case. Your body language is your most powerful communication tool. Just think about this for a moment. If you ask your partner if she will sit down and talk about a concern and she answers, "Sure," while simultaneously shaking her head and rolling her eyes, what will stick out in your mind most? That is right, her body language. She does not want to help! Sometimes these cues are subtle and other times they are forthright, but in either case, your body language is like a picture—it speaks a thousand words.

Body Language

Affirming Body Language	Rejecting Body Language
Hugging	Rolling your eyes
Making eye contact	Making a smirk or grimace
Leaning towards	Shaking your head side to side
Sitting comfortably	Looking away
Smiling	Shrugging your shoulders
Nodding your head	Giving the "evil eye"
up and down	Turning your back

When you are happy and excited, your body language shows it. Your face is graced with a smile, your posture is comfortable and your body radiates a positive glow. When you are frustrated and disappointed, your body language exhibits the opposite characteristics. Your face gets red, your smile turns into a scowl and your body becomes tense.

We are all very good at recognizing our partner's body language, and it is amazing how, without a word said, so much can be stated. For instance, in showing her ongoing disapproval for the amount of TV her husband watches, Sue walks into the living room and stares at him with her arms crossed while shaking her head back and forth. Her husband, Rob, could have many responses to this behavior, but in this case, because this is an ongoing unresolved challenge, he responds negatively by ignoring her and continuing to watch TV. Without a word said, this couple has continued to build tension in their relationship. Each time they repeat this pattern, the more tension and frustration will build and the more difficult it will be to resolve in the future.

What message does your body language send if you walk away from your partner when you're upset? The only way you will know this answer is to discuss this behavior and the feelings and emotions it causes. In this process, you may learn that it does not bother your partner at all. On the other hand, you may discover your partner feels rejected and embarrassed when you walk away. Certainly, this would not be your goal. After all, your intention is to create a win/win situation. As a matter of fact, the only reason you walk away is to avoid saying or doing something you will regret. By having a discussion with your partner, you can better understand each other's behaviors. Perhaps, as a result of your discussion, you may both agree that asking for a time out is an excellent communication tool, but that turning your back and walking away from each other is not.

How you use your body language strongly influences the direction your communication takes you. The more aware you are of how you communicate, the better you can choose your actions. What positive and negative body language habits do you have?

What positive body language habits do you have?
1. _____
2. _____
3. _____
4. _____
5. _____

What negative body language habits do you have?
1. _____
2. _____
3. _____
4. _____
5. _____

If you are not aware you roll your eyes every time you disagree with your partner, you will unknowingly undermine your communication. Your intentions might be good, but if your partner interprets your eye rolling as condescending, you may push your partner away. How can you improve on your non-verbal communication? Perhaps you just want to stop rolling your eyes or quit throwing your hands up in the air when emotionally frustrated. Whatever the case, identify one or two behaviors you want to avoid in your future body language.

Behaviors to avoid:
1. _____
2. _____

To increase your chances of effectively changing your body language, replace your old habits with new ones. Take time to identify what your new habits will be. For example, if you want to stop rolling your eyes, you could switch to an affirmative head nod to let your partner know that you are listening rather than judging.

What new behaviors will you use to replace your old unhealthy ones?

1. _____

2. _____

So often, because we are not aware of the messages our body language sends, we ineffectively communicate. To avoid this make sure the body language you use is purposeful, not accidental.

Tone of Voice

What about the tone of your voice? If a father consistently yells, sooner or later his children will become desensitized to it. However, if he is soft-spoken, but out of urgency, safety or exhaustion raises his voice, the children will stand at attention. This is a great example of how the tone of your voice can influence what messages you send, and certainly this is equally true for your relationship. The following demonstrate the differences between a positive and a negative tone of voice.

Tone of Voice

Affirming Tone of Voice	Rejecting Tone of Voice
Gentle	Harsh
Soft	Loud
Moderately-paced	Fast-paced
Reflective	Judgemental
Reassuring	Blaming
Supportive	Condescending

The difference between tones can be the difference between being supportive or condescending, demanding or inviting, reflective or blaming. It is not necessarily what one says but how it is said that can make the difference in the message. For instance, the statement, "It's okay," could be stated in a loud, condescending tone or a soft, reassuring tone. In either case, it is the same words, but a different message will be received.

How do you think a husband is going to interpret his wife's message when her speech is rushed, loud and condescending? Certainly, he will recognize she is upset, but his reaction may be defensive and argumentative. We have all had this type of experience, where the tone of our partners' voices has created negative emotional reactions in us. It is amazing how the tone of our voices can push each other's emotional buttons.

How are you using your tone of voice to communicate with your partner? What positive and negative tone of voice habits do you have?

What positive tone of voice habits do you have?

1. _____
2. _____
3. _____
4. _____
5. _____

What negative tone of voice habits do you have?

1. _____
2. _____
3. _____
4. _____
5. _____

You can selectively change the pitch, rate, inflection or volume of your voice to get your message across. If you were a professional storyteller, you would use all of these and other techniques to truly engage your listeners. As an expert negotiator, you would consciously select the tone of your voice based on the specific outcome you were looking to accomplish.

When you are seeking to understand your partner, what do you want the tone of your voice to say? This may seem like an elementary question, but more importantly, does your voice demonstrate a supportive or judgmental tone? Take note of your tone, and make sure it is supporting your relationship goal.

Tones of voice to start avoiding:

1. _____
2. _____

How can you improve on the verbal communication of your tones? Perhaps you just want to stop raising your voice and become more supportive. Whatever the case, identify one or two behaviors related to the tone of your voice that you want to avoid in your future communications.

What new behaviors will you use to replace your old unhealthy ones?

1. _____

2. _____

Again, the best way to end an old behavior is by replacing it with a new one. Take a second to identify what new habits you will use to improve the tone of your messages. For instance, perhaps you speak too softly, and are not taken seriously when frustrated. Try to replace this soft tone with a stronger more reflective tone in these situations.

Use the tone of your voice to invite your partner closer to you. Keep an even pace; use an inflective and engaging tone. This will reassure them that you care and are listening. The more comfortable your communication style, the more confidence your partner will feel in sharing his thoughts, feelings and emotions.

Words

Choose your words wisely. If you choose negative, undermining and disrespectful words, your communication will be destructive. On the other hand, choosing supportive and respectful words can improve your communication. There is an old saying that, "Sticks and stones may break my bones but words will never hurt me." Well, we all know this is not true. As a matter of fact, the words people say can leave behind emotional scars that will linger for many years.

If your spouse consistently states that you are smart, attractive and friendly, you are going to feel more positive about yourself. However, if instead the consistent message your partner sends is that you are unattractive and out of shape, you are not going to feel as good about yourself.

What positive or negative words or phrases do you use in your relationship?

What positive words or phrases do you consistently use?
1. _____
2. _____
3. _____
4. _____
5. _____

What negative words or phrases do you use?
1. _____
2. _____
3. _____
4. _____
5. _____

Make a commitment to start replacing these negative habits of yours with new more supportive statements. Again, the best way to end an old behavior is by replacing it with a new one. Therefore, if you say, "How stupid," when your partner makes a mistake, try a more supportive statement or phrase, like, "Don't worry about it; we all make mistakes."

> What new words or phrases will you use to replace your old unhealthy ones?
> 1. _____
> 2. _____

Words are powerful tools for reinforcement. Several years ago, Lisa and I used to get into lively discussions over what direction we were driving. In most cases, she was unaware if we were going north, south, east or west. Knowing my bearings, at any given time, has always come naturally to me. However, for Lisa, it was not something familiar to her. Over time, we would identify our location in relation to major geographic spots in the area such as a town, body of water, mall. Eventually, she became more familiar in identifying her position, in relation to the north, south, east and west. After awhile, I began calling her an "internal compass." Although this was a joke between us, it was also a compliment that reinforced her confidence in directions. Using our words to reinforce behaviors in ourselves and our partners can be very affirming and rewarding.

One of the most common pitfalls in the use of words is generalizations. Generalizations are global, all-inclusive statements which leave no room for exceptions. Consider the following examples:

"All men are insensitive."
"You will never change."
"Women are all the same."
"It does not matter what I do."
"You do not care about anything."

If you say to your partner, "You will never change," you immediately close your eyes to any possible signs of change.

Your words send powerful messages. Be careful of the words you choose, as they may become true.

Generalizations simply do not focus on the topic at hand. If you are "always" lazy, then how can you stop being lazy? I know this may sound like semantics, but your words influence the direction of your communication. How are you going to respond if your partner states that you are "always" lazy? Most likely your immediate feeling is going to be defensive. As a result, your response is likely to be something like this: "I'm not lazy; you are the one who never helps out cleaning the bathrooms." Now, suddenly you are on an entirely different topic.

Avoid generalizations by focusing on your partner's behavior or actions as you explain your thoughts and feelings. For instance, Sue feels that her husband is lazy, and they have gotten into an argument over this time and time again, but nothing ever changes. Now, instead of just telling her husband, Rob, that he is lazy, which tends to start the argument, Sue avoids the generalization by sharing.

> Sue: *After work, you sit and watch TV for two to three hours every evening, while I'm taking care of dinner, the chores and the kids.*
> *I am frustrated because I work hard all day and feel as if I am being taken advantage of.*

> Rob: *I know, but I'm tired and watching TV is relaxing. By no means am I trying to take advantage of you.*

Notice how this message focuses on Sue's thoughts and feelings, and Rob's behavior.

Another excellent way to manage generalization is by repeating them as a question. For instance:

Sue: *You never help out around the house!*
       (Generalization)
Rob: *I never help out around the house?*
       (Repeating the statement as a question)
Sue: *Well, yes, you sometimes help out, but I need*
       more help.
       (Allows your partner to clarify their message)

This technique when stated <u>genuinely and without judgment or defensiveness,</u> will almost always lead your partner to clarify his message. Now instead of responding to the statement "you never help around the house," you can discuss your partner's specific needs.

The words we choose are important, yet at times, we can become caught up in emotions and feelings. When this happens, we become less selective with the words we choose. This can lead to making a situation worse than it already is. It is not a bad idea to take a time out to think before your emotions carry you away. If necessary, write down your thoughts and feelings. This will allow you to better understand yourself and enable you to effectively choose words that are more thoughtful and helpful. You can later review the situation with your partner after some of the emotional tension has dissipated (see Emotional Awareness exercise Chapter Five).

Congruency
Taking ownership for the messages you send and receive is very important. This can be accomplished by being congruent with your body language, tone of voice and words. When these work in tandem, they send very clear messages. When they do not, communication often becomes filled with mixed messages.

We have all been told, "You are not listening." Yet, for most of us, our first response to this is, "Yes, I am." Telling your partner that you are listening does not mean you are. Even if you feel like you are listening, if your partner does not feel you are, then your perception is irrelevant. Your partner needs to feel that you are listening. One of the most common reasons for your partner feeling that you are not listening is that you are not congruent with your body language, tone of voice and words. Perhaps you are listening with your ears, but you are not looking at your partner or responding with an affirmative head nod. Therefore, your partner's perception is that you are not listening. Another reason your partner may feel you are not listening is because you have not summarized his/her message. Instead you quickly responded with your own opinion.

To listen is to associate with your body language, be acknowledging in your words and reflective in your voice. When all three of these do not work in tandem, then you are incongruent and send a mixed message. Regardless of intent, you will not be perceived as listening. Remember, communication is a process of sending and receiving information. The perspective we need to take as speakers in communication is simple: the only message sent is that which is heard. Therefore, if our partners have not received our intended messages, we need to try to communicate these messages differently and ask for their help in understanding.

One of the purposes of healthy communication is making sure that the correct message has been both sent and received. If you are asked to help make dinner and your answer is, "Okay," while shrugging your shoulders, then you have sent an incongruent message. If you find yourself sending an incongruent message, stop and align your communication tools. If you do not feel like cooking, send a clear message. Make eye contact, use a supportive tone and explain that you would prefer to order out rather than to cook a meal and clean up afterwards. From this clear point, you can negotiate with your partner. Perhaps your partner wants to save a little cash for the weekend and would prefer to do all the cooking and cleaning that evening. Or, perhaps your partner is happy to order out. In either case, clear communication can lead to a mutual decision being reached.

Unfortunately, your partner will not always send congruent messages and neither will you. When this is the case, try to avoid reacting to the incongruence with frustration. As a listener, take responsibility for seeking out the message your partner intends to communicate, rather than the first one you interpret. If your partner rolls his eyes and shakes his head while agreeing to your question, seek clarification.

> Sally: *Ron, I am not sure what your needs are. Help me understand.*

Asking for clarity in a supportive tone gives your partner the opportunity to clarify his/her message and helps you understand what your partner is really thinking or feeling. So often couples skip this step and assume they know what their partners intended. As you know, assuming is not the best policy. More often than not, when conflict exists, the first message you interpret is not the intended one. By not seeking clarification, there is a great chance that you will misunderstand each other. This will send you down the wrong path, and you will have to do a lot of back-tracking to get back on track.

How do you increase your level of congruence?

First and foremost, you need to recognize congruence as an important part of your relationship. Second, take time to observe your behaviors, words and tone of voice. Identify a few areas where or when you are not congruent. Work on improving these areas one at a time and stay conscious in your desire to be congruent. When you are not congruent, take responsibility by acknowledging your thoughts, feelings or actions with your partner.

> Sally: *I'm sorry, but I did not say that right. Let me try it again.*
>
> OR
>
> Ron: *I'm sorry. I was rolling my eyes. Can I start over?*

These simple statements accomplish several objectives. First and foremost, they let you take responsibility. Second, they unequivocally tell your partner that you sent the wrong message and are committed to sending it more clearly. Third, they keep your partner on task by asking for permission to start over. It is by paying attention and practicing these types of interactions that you will become more congruent.

SUMMARY POINTS

Communication is constant and it affects your relationship whether you are talking or not. By improving your body language, tone of voice and word choice, you empower your communication. The more focused and congruent your message, the clearer and more effective your communication will become.

Self-Assessment Questions:
- ❑ How do I use my body language to send clear messages?
- ❑ How do I choose the tone of my voice to effectively communicate with my partner?
- ❑ Is my word selection generally positive or negative?

❑ Which area of communication do I need to improve on the most: body language, voice, words or congruency?
❑ Which area of communication do I perform the best with: body language, voice, words or congruency?
❑ Am I congruent in my messages?

Moving Forward

Using your body language, tone of voice and words congruently is important. However, healthy communication takes much more than these tools. In the next chapter we will discuss the skill of understanding first and how paraphrasing and clarifying questions can further enhance your communication with your partner. Ultimately, this will improve the clarity of the messages you send and receive.

CHAPTER EIGHT

Understand First

*"People seldom improve when they have no other model
but themselves to copy after."*
—Oliver Goldsmith

When it comes to communication, there is perhaps no more important fundamental value than feeling understood and respected. Those couples who incorporate the philosophy of understanding first into their daily communication experience less tension and frustration when faced with different challenges. The key focus of understanding first is to create a safe environment during your communication. Therefore, this chapter will focus on the following three concepts.

✓ Creating a safe environment
✓ Understanding first
✓ Getting back on track once you have fallen off

Creating a Safe Environment

One of the most important goals of healthy communication is creating a safe environment. Contrary to what many people think, understanding your partner has nothing to do with agreeing with each other. After all, it is not necessary, nor is it possible to always agree with one another. It is absolutely critical that you respect each other by listening. For instance, your partner may want to paint all the rooms in the house a new color. Even though you disagree with the idea, make it an obligation to listen to and acknowledge your partner's thoughts and feelings. This process may take a little more time, but both you and your partner will walk away feeling respected and appreciated regardless of the final decision. Reaching this state is much more important than whether or not you paint the inside of the house. How partners respond to and interact with each other determines whether they create a safe, nurturing environment or one that is uncomfortable or volatile. The following interaction demonstrates how quickly an emotionally unsafe environment can be created.

Creating an unsafe environment

Statement:	*Do not raise your voice at me, I feel uncomfortable when you do.*
Response:	*Don't be so sensitive! I'm not yelling!*

It does not take many negative responses like this one to teach you not to disclose your thoughts and feelings. The more this happens, the more you will hold back and the less emotional intimacy will develop between you and your partner. It is difficult enough to make your interpersonal thoughts and feelings vulnerable to another's review, but without a safe environment it becomes nearly impossible. Here is an example of how to create a safe environment.

Creating a safe environment

Statement:	*Do not raise your voice at me, I feel uncomfortable when you do.*
Response:	*I am sorry. I did not mean to yell. I have had a bad day and I am frustrated.*

Or

I am sorry. I did not realize I was getting so loud.

In what direction is this conversation moving? The more comfortable you are with your partner's response to your interpersonal thoughts, feelings and wants, the safer you will feel to share. Imagine for a minute, how either of the above messages could be further enhanced for the better or intensified for the worse depending on the tone of voice and body language used.

As you can imagine, creating a safe environment is what a good friendship is all about. With a friend, you aren't afraid to share your most personal thoughts and feelings. Your relationship should be no different.

Is your relationship a safe haven for your thoughts and feelings?

When you have something important to discuss with your partner, and it is going to cause discomfort, ease the pressure of the discussion by creating a safe environment first. A key step to accomplishing this is to acknowledge your concerns up front, such as:

"Honey, I have a difficult topic we need to talk through, and it's not going to be easy for either of us. I am not sure where to start, so if you can bear with me I would greatly appreciate it."

This congruent, honest approach prepares both of you for what is going to come next. So often in our communication we start with judgments, blaming and accusations. This makes our partner defensive and we begin to throw emotional darts at one another rather than focus on listening.

A safe environment is not something you earn for a lifetime. It is something you continually invest in and build day after day and year after year. Certainly, the more times you successfully reach an understanding, the easier it becomes; however, it is not something that happens automatically because of love. As a matter of fact, working to achieve it will not come without its share of mistakes. Luckily, you will be given many opportunities to create a safe environment. The key to creating a safe environment is to understand first.

Understanding First

In order to create a safe environment, your fundamental focus should be to understand your partner first. Unfortunately, understanding does not always happen first. For instance:

Elizabeth:	*My drive home from work today was terrible. It took me an extra twenty minutes.*
Gary:	*Mine was even worse. I swear, no one knows how to drive in this town. There were two accidents and some road work going on that really backed up traffic.*
Elizabeth:	*My drive is already fifteen minutes longer than your drive.*
Gary:	*The road work will be going on for the next two months. It is not going to be fun.*

Can you imagine how this can go on? It is like talking about fishing stories. As each shares, the stories get longer and the fish bigger. This "verbal ping-pong" is very common and does create some camaraderie when the topic is neutral. This approach involves no active listening skills. For instance, in the example above neither Gary's or Elizabeth's thoughts or feelings were acknowledged. This is perfectly fine when partners are telling stories or sharing general information. However, when the topic turns to something important like your thoughts or feelings on spending time together, then "verbal ping-pong" can quickly turn into "verbal jousting." For example:

Simon:	*I'm going out with some people from work tonight.*
Rachael:	*You spend too much time out with them.*
Simon:	*I do not get out that much!*
Rachael:	*Yes you do!*
Simon:	*You always complain when I go out!*
Rachael:	*You do not spend enough time at home.*
Simon:	*I did not go anywhere last week.*
Rachael:	*That's not the point.*
Simon:	*Then don't complain about it.*

This "verbal jousting" does not focus on the real issue, and the couple only becomes more frustrated with one another. As a result, there is no resolution, and the negative pattern continues. This is why you need to understand your partner first. Rather than getting caught up in "verbal jousting," seek out the meat or meaning of your partner's thoughts and feelings. *As a listener, you have to focus on what your partner is trying to say, and as a speaker, you have to focus on sending your intended message.*

Lisa and I were not always good at understanding each other at first; as a matter of fact, for a few years I do not think we knew we were even supposed to. Instead, our time and energy focused on explaining or defending our personal position as the example above does.

Today, we are much better at listening to each other. It is important to us and something we continually strive to improve upon. This is one of the biggest factors in our success and any couples long-term satisfaction.

Hearing is passive; but listening is active. To hear someone means little when it comes to communication. It requires no active interest or intent. Listening, however, is quite different. To listen is to acknowledge your partner's thoughts, feelings and actions. It is to be associated, congruent and involved in the conversation. There are two communication skills that will help you become a better listener. These are paraphrasing and clarifying questions.

Paraphrasing

Paraphrasing is a process of repeating back to your partner what you have heard. Another common term for paraphrasing is reflective listening. Paraphrasing allows you to summarize what you think was said and invite your partner to clarify any misunderstanding. This is very important because what you think you heard is not necessarily what your partner intended to say. Paraphrasing gives you the opportunity to insure there is no miscommunication before moving on in your conversation. Achieving this requires you to set aside your own judgments, thoughts and feelings. Through paraphrasing, your primary goal is to acknowledge your partner's thoughts and feelings. Reaching this state does not require you to agree with your partner. It just requires you to acknowledge their thoughts and feelings. In doing this, you send a clear, undeniable message that you understand and respect them. Once you have accomplished this, your partner will almost immediately feel more comfortable and less defensive. As a result, they are able to turn their focus onto your thoughts, feelings and needs. It is this reciprocal interaction that fosters healthy communication. The following examples demonstrate this process.

Healthy communication through paraphrasing
>Statement: *I am scared about the interview.*
>Paraphrase: *You are feeling a little nervous.*
>OR
>Statement: *You are more interested in watching TV than in me.*
>Paraphrase: *You feel I care more about the TV than you.*

It is not necessary to repeat the exact words to adequately paraphrase. The real goal is in matching the intended message. Each of these paraphrases does just that, they acknowledge the thoughts and feelings of the speaker. As always, you want to avoid making judgments or opinions. Instead, concentrate on being genuine and sincerely interested in your partner by sending a congruent message that reflects their thoughts and feelings.

The following examples illustrate how easily one's response can lead towards unhealthy communication.

Unhealthy communication (defensiveness)
>Statement: *I am scared about the interview.*
>Response: *Get over it; it's just an interview.*
>OR
>Statement: *You are more interested in watching TV than in me.*
>Response: *Oh—give it a break, you are always complaining about the TV.*

As you can imagine, these responses not only fail to acknowledge your partner's thoughts and feelings, but they become barriers between you. To effectively paraphrase, you need to step back emotionally, putting aside your own wants, needs and expectations and instead focus on your partner's thoughts, feelings and actions.

Take time to practice paraphrasing every chance you get. This can be with your spouse, kids, friends, parents, co-workers or anyone for that matter. It is important to get comfortable with paraphrasing through practice. The last thing you want to do is attempt paraphrasing in the middle of a heated disagreement without the comfort of having any past success.

It can also be helpful to set up some expectations around listening. I know many couples who have agreed, in advance, that if either of them does not feel heard, all he or she has to do is let the other know. Once this happens, each of them becomes responsible for slowing down and listening until they both feel understood. If you have not already established a similar agreement, now would be an ideal time.

Clarifying questions

Clarifying questions help you gather additional information so you can better understand your partner's message and paraphrase it more effectively. Clarifying questions can be either open-ended or close-ended. Open-ended questions request the speaker to share more details about her thoughts and feelings, while close-ended questions require a simple, brief answer. Below are examples of open-ended questions.

Open-ended clarifying questions

Why do you feel I do not understand?
How can I help you?
What have I done to upset you?
How did you manage to accomplish that?
How would you like me to hang the picture?
What do you need?
What specifically did you not like about the food?

The following discussion demonstrates how open-ended questions and paraphrasing work together.

> Statement: *You do not help around the house!*
> Open-ended: *What would you like me to do differently?*
> Response: *Clean the kitchen and the bathrooms every weekend.*
> Open-ended: *What specifically would you like me to do in the kitchen and bathrooms?*
> Response: *Wash the dishes, floors, countertops, shower and toilets.*
> Paraphrase: *By cleaning the dishes, floors, countertops, as well as the shower and toilets every weekend, you would be happy?*
> Response: *Yes, that would be a great help.*

You can see how the open-ended questions can help you clarify specifically what your partner's needs are, and paraphrasing allows you to acknowledge those needs, wants or expectations. As a result, positive contact is made, and problem-solving can occur.

Close-ended questions are also an excellent means to gather and clarify information.

Close-ended clarifying questions

Do you think we talk enough?
Do you like this color?
Do you want to go out to eat?
Can I help you?
Would you like me to fix the garbage disposal?
Are you happy?

Close-ended questions are often answered with just a few words. If you want to know how old Tommy is, you would ask, "How old are you, Tommy?" His answer would be simply, "I'm twelve." Asking close-ended questions will not gather much detail, but they have their uses. They are very good at extracting specific information, for instance:

Close-ended: *Are you mad at me?*
Response: *Yes!*

From this response you could follow up with open-ended questions to gather more information and understand your partner.

Open-ended: *What specifically are you mad about?*

This open-ended question will surely help you understand your partner in more detail. Using both paraphrasing and clarifying questions will dramatically improve your communication. Take the following example for instance:

Statement: *I feel that you are more interested in watching TV than in me. (Angry)*
Clarifying: *Why do you feel that way? (Open-ended: acknowledging)*
Response: *We have talked about this several times. (Frustrated)*
Summary: *So, you feel that nothing ever changes. (Close-ended; serves to both paraphrase and acknowledge)*
Response: *Yes! (Feels heard and acknowledged)*
Sharing: *I guess I just like to relax at night and to me that means watching TV. (Sharing personal information)*

Paraphrase: *I know you work hard and like to take a break at night. It's just that it seems we do not get any time together. (Understanding)*

Response: *Well, let's come up with some agreement that meets both of our needs. (Starting to problem-solve)*

Response: *That would be great. (Agreement)*

It is from healthy discussions like this that couples can begin problem-solving. Without understanding taking place, a couple can get caught arguing over personalities or the TV instead of the real issue of spending enough time together.

This next example verifies how not using paraphrasing and clarifying questions can quickly lead to a misunderstanding.

Statement: *I feel that you are more interested in watching TV than in me. (Concern)*

Reaction: *Oh! Give it a break, you are always complaining about the TV. (Frustration)*

Statement: *You do not care about anyone but yourself! (Frustration)*

Response: *You're the one that's never happy. (Anger)*

Can you imagine how this conversation might grow? Unfortunately, it does not take more than a few seconds for us to start misunderstanding each other. I hope you can see the value of using clarifying questions and how they work together with paraphrasing to help you understand your partner. Not only will these skills allow you to create a safe environment, but they will also make a positive emotional connection between your partner and you.

One of the common goals in a healthy relationship is

building a sense of confidence in each other. Partners need to have confidence in each other; they need to know that when things get tough, they will work together, rather than against each other. Paraphrasing and clarifying questions used in tandem with healthy body language, words and tone of voice will help you reach this goal.

There is an inherent emotional risk in sharing that we all must take. Upon sharing, we automatically subject ourselves to the possible negative reactions of our partner. If they laugh, tell us we are stupid or jump to conclusions without first understanding us, we will become less and less comfortable sharing. These types of negative responses close down communication and prevent couples from learning and growing together. This negative interaction can be avoided when partners are committed to creating a safe environment for each to share thoughts, feelings and actions.

Getting Back on Track Once You Have Fallen Off

As much as we would like to communicate right the first time, this does not always happen. From time to time, we will get caught in both verbal and emotional jousting. When this happens, we simply need to get back on track. This is not easy, however. Once jousting starts, we can become more committed to our cause and become less willing to listen. I am certainly no stranger to this situation, but have learned over time that the longer Lisa and I wait to get back on track, the harder it becomes and the less happy we are.

An important step for getting back on track is recognizing that you are off track in the first place. This may sound obvious, but in many cases, due to your emotional investment, it is not always easy to recognize this. Here is where your emotional awareness can help. You need to be able to identify the signs of losing emotionally. The quicker you can identify the physical, mental and emotional clues of losing, the faster you can recognize that you have fallen off track. In addition, by keeping your relationship vision in your forethought, you can more quickly remember the type of emotional environment you are seeking. Once you have fallen off track and recognize it, the best thing you can do is acknowledge it to your partner. For instance:

"John, I (we) have gotten off track and need to get back on before it's too late. Can I (we) start over?"

This level of sharing is not always easy. Therefore, many couples use distraction techniques such as a time-out or breaking the emotional cycle to get refocused. Discussing past failures and successes, at a neutral time, also enables you to make advanced decisions on what you will do if you are losing emotionally. I know many couples who have agreed in advance to slow down and start listening whenever they get off track. These not-so-little lessons are very important components in building a healthy relationship.

What tricks have you learned to help your relationship get back on track?

1. _____
2. _____
3. _____
4. _____
5. _____

Understanding first is a very powerful communication skill, and achieving it requires determination, persistence and dedication. There are many benefits of understanding first, such as feeling respected, appreciated and understood. As a result, your relationship's emotional intimacy builds and the bond between you deepens.

The more unhealthy independent or unhealthy dependent characteristics you and your partner carry, the more difficult it will be for you to understand first. These characteristics will block you from understanding and instead you will defend (unhealthy independence) or you will avoid getting your needs met (unhealthy dependence). In either case, by building your level of interdependence you will enhance your ability to understand first and in doing so you will create a positive emotional connection.

SUMMARY POINTS

Understanding first should be the goal of your communication, and creating a safe environment is the main vehicle for accomplishing this. By acknowledging each other's thoughts, feelings, needs and expectations, you will resolve many differences. Unfortunately, many couples do not understand each other or the problem before attempting to resolve it. This is equivalent to running a marathon without any training. Please do not let this happen to you. Practice understanding each other with every opportunity you get. Paraphrasing and clarifying questions are key components to understanding and allow you to communicate more effectively together.

Self-Assessment Questions:
- ❏ What does it mean to understand first?
- ❏ How do I currently create a safe emotional environment in my relationship?
- ❏ How does paraphrasing help me understand my partner better?
- ❏ How often do I use clarifying questions to better understand my partner?

Moving Forward

Understanding first is a fundamental component of healthy communication. So often, we do not take the time to fully understand each other before we start problem-solving. We need to avoid making wrong turns like this and instead make right turns in our relationship. The next chapter will show you how understanding first is an important component of problem-solving.

CHAPTER NINE

Problem-Solving

"Tolerance is the oil
which takes the friction out of life."
—*Wilbert E. Scheer*

Problem-solving is an important step to managing the many challenges that will arise in your relationship. When carried out correctly, problem-solving should allow you to reach mutually-agreeable decisions. The skills we will discuss are helpful in managing all of your rules (preferences, negotiables and boundaries). However, the focus of this chapter will be on effectively managing your negotiables since we had previously discussed in Chapter Six how to manage your preferences and boundaries.

The most common types of negotiables you face involve making decisions and balancing differences, such as: Whether you rent or buy a home? How will you maintain your health? What are your communication standards? When do you buy a new car? Will you have kids? What type of vacations will you go on? What type of sexual intimacy do you want to build? How will you manage your money? How will you manage trust and honesty?

Sometimes, your negotiables are in response to situations or dilemmas in which you find yourself. For instance: What do you do if a fire destroys your home? What will you do if you lose your job? How will you manage if you can not have kids, but want them? What will you do if your teenage daughter gets pregnant? What type of religious affiliation will you have? How will you manage the death of a parent or sibling? What will you do if your spouse becomes a substance abuser?

These are only a few examples of the many obstacles that you might face in your relationship. Each one requires managing different situations, thoughts, feelings, wants, needs and expectations.

Every couple manages its problems differently based on their personality characteristics, level of interdependence, emotional awareness, knowledge base, communication skills, and past experiences. It is important to remember that there is no "cookie cutter" approach to problem-solving. Some couples get loud and kick furniture before they can sit down to resolve differences, while others get quiet first. Some couples can work through differences almost immediately, while others need several hours, days, weeks or months in order to reach mutually-acceptable agreements.

Even though there is no perfect process for working together, there is a clear goal and that is to reach *mutually-acceptable decisions*. This is not always an easy task, but your chances for success can increase when the following three skills are incorporated into your problem-solving process.

✓ Understand first
✓ Take an "us" versus the "problem" approach
✓ Compromise and accommodate

The above skills provide a solid frame of reference to work from regardless of the problem, and they can occur in any order or all at once. Once we have reviewed each of these we will demonstrate how they work together to help reach mutually-acceptable decisions.

Understand First

Both you and your partner need to have your thoughts, feelings, wants, needs or expectations validated and acknowledged. This is equally true, if one of you has just lost your job or if you have a difference of opinion on which refrigerator to purchase. As discussed previously, understanding first is accomplished by sincerely listening and understanding your partner first. Using clarifying questions and paraphrasing along with congruent messages will help acknowledge your partner and create a safe environment in which this can happen, even when you disagree.

Sometimes, writing down your thoughts, feelings, needs and expectations can enhance the process of understanding first and then problem-solving. It is not necessary to write several pages. Five to ten minutes is often more than enough time for each of you to write down your perspectives. From this point, you can take a few minutes to understand each other first. If you have never tried writing your thoughts and feelings down, give it a chance. Many couples find it helps clarify their positions and gets them better focused on the solution, rather than on the problem. Certainly, it is not necessary to go through this process every time you have a difference in opinion, need to make a decision or find yourself facing an unusual challenge. However, there are times when it can make the difference between effective problem-solving or getting stuck.

When seeking to understand, be sure to recognize any other influencing factors (dreams, hopes, expectations, past experiences or emotions) that may be impacting one another's decision. For example, John and Sandy are in the market for a new computer, and Sandy feels she has found the best deal, but John disagrees. By using clarifying questions and paraphrasing, Sandy discovers that John had a negative experience with the maker of the computer she likes. This factor helps Sandy understand why John is so strongly against her choice, and she can more easily problem-solve with him.

Take an "Us" Versus the "Problem" Approach

In the process of problem-solving, you want to make sure you and your partner are on the same side. When the problem lies between you, you are in opposition. In this case, one of you is right and the other is wrong. It's difficult to problem-solve from these positions. Make sure to take an *"us" versus the "problem"* approach, rather than a *"you" versus "me"* approach. Turn the problem into a challenge that you can solve together. For example:

> *"We both have different needs; let's focus on how we can manage these differences together."*

Taking this type of an approach puts partners on the same side, which makes problem-solving more of a discussion than an argument. When taking an "us" versus the "problem" approach, make sure to include the following steps:

1. *Take ownership of your thoughts and feelings by using "I"*: "I felt disappointed when you did not call when running late," rather than the second person "you." For instance, "You made me feel disappointed when you did not call me when running late."
2. *Focus on your partner's behavior*: "You did not call when running late."
3. *Avoid generalizations*: "You do not care about me."
4. *Focus on a solution*: "Call me when you're running over fifteen minutes late, so I will know everything is okay."

Compromise and Accommodate

Perhaps the biggest key to problem-solving is learning that reciprocity is accomplished through compromising and accommodating. Each partner must give and take in order to reach mutual decisions. We are all familiar with compromising and accommodating. After all, they are key components of managing preferences. On the other hand, sometimes our accommodation is more intentional, like going to the football game with your spouse, without making a fuss, even though it is not your favorite thing to do. The opposite of compromising would be rigidity, and the backbone of your relationship will be broken unless it is flexible. Reaching mutual decisions without compromising and accommodating is impossible.

Once a mutual agreement has been reached, both partners are obligated to hold themselves accountable to it. This is where many individuals get their relationships in trouble. Instead of sticking to their agreement, one or both of them break it. Sticking to your agreements will increase the validity of the process and increase the effectiveness of your problem-solving.

Reaching Mutually-Acceptable Decisions

To illustrate the process of problem-solving, we will examine a very common negotiable: buying a new car. Let's see how understanding first, taking an "us" versus the "problem" approach, and compromising and accommodating can lead to a mutual decision. To more clearly delineate the process of problem-solving, we will use two examples. In the first example, a couple wants to buy a new car, and in the second example, only one partner is interested in buying a new car.

Example #1:
Bill and Marilyn have been thinking about a new car for several months, and have decided that now is the time to buy

one. In this case, right from the start, they are taking an *us-ver-sus-the-problem* approach. Both have a desire to buy a new car and only need to figure out the details of making their purchase.

To start working out the details, they begin by *under-standing first*, so the thoughts, feelings, wants, needs and expectations of each can be understood. As a result, they discuss the following: how much to spend, what manufacturer, model, accessories, color, who will negotiate the sale, whether to trade in their old car, buy an extended warranty, finance or lease and for how many years.

In an effort to more clearly identify each other's thoughts, feelings, wants, needs and expectations, Bill and Marilyn wrote them down.

Preferences for a new car	Bill's	Marilyn's
Cost	$20,000-$25,000	$23,000-28,000
Model	Camry	Camry
Make	Toyota	Toyota
Accessories	No Preference	Premium package
Color	White	Does not matter
Payment options	Lease	Finance 5 years
Trade In or Sell	Trade In	Trade In
Extra warranties	No Preference	None
Who will negotiate	Me	You

After understanding each other and writing their thoughts and feelings down, Bill and Marilyn have many common wants and needs. The only difference they have to decide on is whether to finance or lease. To make this discussion easier, they identify the pros and cons of each and begin clarifying their differences.

Lease	
Pros	**Cons**
No down payment necessary	Will have to trade the car in after the lease is up or buy it
Lower monthly payments	Will build no equity
Will always have a newer car	
No major maintenance concerns	
Can have more options with a lower price	

Finance	
Pros	**Cons**
Low interest rates right now	Can not afford desired car
Will save money in the long run	Will have to deal with more long-term maintenace issues
Will own the car when payments are completed	
Could sell later for next down payment	

After reviewing the pros and cons, Bill and Marilyn began *compromising and accommodating* until a mutual decision was reached. In this case, they agree to finance the car for sixty months and since neither has a strong preference towards any extra warranties, they pass on the option. They also purchase the premium package because they are able to do so in Bill's price range. They decide to trade in their old car and finance a white Toyota Camry, with a premium accessory package.

As you can see from this example, problem-solving is an ongoing process of breaking down larger thoughts, feelings and actions into smaller pieces. These smaller pieces are easier to understand, acknowledge and manage.

In this scenario, the process was pretty uneventful and straightforward. We have all experienced times when problem-solving meets very little resistance and teamwork prevails. As discussed before, it is not always necessary to write everything out; just understanding each other is often enough. However, when faced with more difficult decisions, writing things down can be very helpful.

Example #2:

In this scenario, Paul wants to buy a new car and his wife, Judy, is strongly opposed to the idea. Instead of being in agreement, right from the start they are on opposite sides. In this case, Judy and Paul need to understand each other's thoughts, feelings, wants, needs and expectations.

| Thoughts, Feelings, Needs, Wants and Expectations ||
Paul's	Judy's
I have waited long enough	We have other bills to pay
All my friends are getting new cars	Your friends are not going to make our payments
We can afford a car due to my last raise	It's an added expense since our current car runs fine
I've never had a new car	We need to save our money for an annual family vacation

Paul and Judy discuss each of these differences until both feel understood and respected. However, reaching this point is not easy, and they get into an argument over Paul's habit of spending money without involving Judy. They have had this conversation more than once, and each time they become more frustrated with each other. However, after two weeks of discussions, they come to a mutually-acceptable agreement. They agree not to make purchases over one hundred dollars without consulting each other first. It is not until this issue is effectively addressed that they are able to continue forward with the discussion of buying a new car.

Through their ongoing discussions, it also becomes evident that Judy has a need to go on an annual vacation. Paul, therefore, confirms his suspicions by acknowledging her thoughts and feelings.

Paul:	*Judy, if we can save up for and go on a yearly family vacation, would it be okay to buy a new car?*
Judy:	*That might be okay.*

Clearly, Paul and Judy are feeling more comfortable, are on the same side and can start discussing where they could compromise and accommodate to reach a mutual decision.

Compromise and Accommodate	
Wait a year	Reduce casual spending
Buy a standard model	Save a down payment
Save money by canceling cable TV	Go on a nice vacation every other year
Pick up an extra shift a month	Buy a nice used car

After much discussion, Judy and Paul come to the mutual agreement that they will wait a year, save up a larger down payment, take a family vacation every other year and Paul will cancel cable and work an extra shift each month. Not only are Paul and Judy satisfied with this outcome, but they have also resolved a long-standing problem about how much money either could spend without first consulting the other.

Clearly, you have found yourself in opposition with your partner. These situations represent opportunities to build respect, appreciation and ultimately, intimacy in your relationship. Understanding first, taking an us-versus-the-problem stance and learning how to compromise are the mechanics for problem-solving and can be applied to many situations, events and circumstances. They are equally helpful whether you are trying to resolve your parenting differences, improve your sexual relationship, or manage the household responsibilities. Using these skills effectively takes time, patience and persistence, but once you understand how to use them, they will allow you to resolve your greatest relationship challenges.

Is Problem-Solving Really This Easy?

From these examples, it would appear that problem-solving is a relatively straightforward process. When following the directions for making cookies, you find that all recipes are not the same. Some are very easy and almost foolproof, while others require exact steps such as sifting the flour or following a specific order for adding each ingredient. Problem-solving is much the same. Sometimes the process is relatively simple and requires minimal effort to reach a mutual decision. At other times, there are many factors that make the task difficult. Often these barriers are other unresolved preferences, negotiables or boundaries. For instance, the negotiable of how much money they could spend without consultation prevented Paul and Judy from discussing a new car purchase. They first had to resolve this long-standing issue. Preferences are another cause for poor problem-solving. If a couple has not learned how to accommodate and compromise the little things, these will slowly chip away at the relationship's emotional intimacy. Likewise, unresolved boundaries also reduce a couple's effectiveness with problem-solving.

In looking back at what we have discussed in previous chapters, there are several other factors that influence our problem-solving abilities.

- Interdependence
- Emotional awareness
- Communication skills
- Past experiences and future expectations
- Relationship vision

Interdependence

Some of us have such strong dependent or independent characteristics that we have a hard time effectively sharing and understanding. Overly-independent partners continue to expound, and hold onto their own thoughts, feelings, needs, wants and expectations, rather than listen to and understand their partner's. The overly-dependent partners, on the other hand, are unable to effectively contribute to the process. They are too quick to defer their thoughts, feelings, needs, wants and expectations, due to their own inhibition. Either approach increases the time necessary to reach a resolution and contributes to the frustration level. One needs to be as interdependent as possible to problem-solve effectively.

Emotional awareness

Some people are emotionally-insecure and are ineffective at sharing with or understanding their partners, especially when in disagreement. Due to a high level of emotional sensitivity, they either avoid or engage in conflict as a means of managing it. This protective mode only serves to further distance them from themselves and their partners. This lack of emotional integrity prevents them from making themselves vulnerable to their own and others' real thoughts and feelings. As a result, an understanding cannot be reached.

Communication skills

Some couples have not developed healthy communication skills such as being congruent, paraphrasing, and using clarifying questions. Instead, they send mixed messages and filter information in ineffective ways. They may have all the right intentions, but they do not know how to obtain good outcomes. They continue to apply the same ineffective solutions to their problems even though the results are less than desired. A good example of this would be continuing to argue over preferences or being sarcastic with your spouse even though you know it only makes matters worse.

Past experiences and future expectations

The past is often seen as a reflection of the future. When a couple consistently has difficulty with an issue, eventually it becomes a predictable pattern in their relationship. For example, you may know that every time there is a discussion about your husband's parents, an argument is going to break out between you. The more often this occurs, the quicker you become at pushing each other's buttons. At some point, these past experiences begin dictating future expectations. Just thinking about the topic brings up emotional tension. Therefore, when you attempt to problem-solve, part of you has already given up and is looking for any sign that it is not going to work out. This reduces your chance for problem-solving. Even if you are really committed to seeking a resolution, it will take you longer than you would like, and you will experience discomfort in getting there. It is this discomfort that causes us to lose focus.

Relationship vision

Some couples and individuals do not understand what they are trying to accomplish in their relationships. They have no relationship vision. They do not know they are trying to build a healthy environment where differences can be expressed without negative consequences. This lack of focus blurs the lines of commitment and respect, making the goals of communication and problem-solving vague and nearly unattainable.

Putting it All Together

With all this said, can you become a more effective problem-solver? Yes, so long as you are willing to acknowledge and understand your personal strengths and weaknesses. You can become more interdependent. You can build more emotional awareness. You can increase your knowledge base and develop better skill sets. You can develop a clear relationship vision. Yet, even with these in place, you will face normal ups and downs that will challenge your problem-solving skills.

In general, the means to problem-solving are not as important as reaching a mutually-acceptable agreement. The less painful the process, the safer each partner will feel and ultimately, the easier the process will become. Become efficient as possible by reducing the time and negative energy it takes, and you will be better off as a couple. To do this, avoid comparing yourself to other couples, as some will be more effective and others less effective than you are. Instead, understand the time and energy it takes you today to resolve differences and set a benchmark. If it currently takes you two weeks to work through an argument, establish a mutual goal to build in the elements we have discussed and reduce the time to a week and a half. This is a dramatic improvement from where you started out. By continuing these efforts, you can eventually work the process down to a week and eventually to a few days or even a few hours.

167

It is important at this point to remember not every difference or situation will be resolved in mutually-satisfying ways. Sometimes the outcome of your discussion will be a lose-lose proposition. This is only natural and should not be equated as failure. This is especially true with boundaries because they are non-negotiable. Fortunately, a vast majority of the difficult situations we find ourselves in can be successfully managed by understanding first, taking an us-versus-the-problem stance, and compromising and accommodating one another.

SUMMARY POINTS

Problem-solving is something all couples face and is something to focus on and constantly improve on. With each success, your trust, confidence and respect will grow for each other. The examples we used are universal. They reflect thousands of potential problems that can occur in your relationship. Yet, the skills to resolve them all remain the same: understand first, create a win-win environment by taking an us-versus-the-problem approach and eventually you will be able to compromise and accommodate each other. Through these efforts, you can reach mutually-acceptable decisions.

Self-Assessment Questions:
- ❑ How good am I at problem-solving?
- ❑ Do I listen first by acknowledging my partner's thoughts and feelings?
- ❑ How do I work with my partner to make mutual decisions?
- ❑ How well do I accommodate and compromise?
- ❑ Where is my greatest opportunity for improving my problem-solving skills?

❑ When tension builds, does perseverance towards the goal win, or do I get lost in the process?

Moving Forward

The first step of problem-solving is to reach mutually-agreeable decisions. In most cases, this is all that a couple must do in order to resolve differences. However, sometimes problem-solving requires going a few steps further to create actual changes in your partner and yourself. Accomplishing this is the next step to *Making Right Turns in Your Relationship.*

CHAPTER TEN

Creating Change

"Our patience will achieve more than our force."
—*Edmund Burke*

To a certain degree, we all want to change something about our partners, our relationships and ourselves, all of which we believe will bring more satisfaction and less tension to our lives. Even though many motivational speakers and self-proclaimed experts promote "instant change," I do not. Change is a process, not an event. It is true that taking the time to reach a mutually-agreeable decision can create change in and of itself. However, many improvements in your relationship will take additional steps to break your existing habits or start new ones.

A common perception that undermines many relationships is the belief that once an issue has been discussed and agreed upon, everything will work out. I only wish this were the case, but it is not. Reaching a mutually-agreeable decision is only part of the process. Actually creating change is where most of the work occurs. For instance, your partner and you may agree to be more supportive of each other, but your ingrained skills and habits do not automatically change. To be successful, you will both need to break old habits and acquire new ones. This takes time and energy to accomplish.

The process of creating change comes with its share of ups and downs. The goal however, does not change due to these fluctuations. To create any successful change, you will need to work together, traversing the many different distractions that come between you, without losing track of your goal. In today's society of quick fixes, seeing change as a process may not be too appealing, but its long-term positive impact will far outlast any short-term gain from a quick fix. This philosophy is similar to how a healthy lifestyle of diet and exercise (long-term goal) will be more effective at controlling your weight than the diet of the month (short-term goal) will be.

To help you make effective changes in your life and relationship, we will review the components of change which allow this to happen.

The Process of Creating Change

There are five components that occur during the process of creating change. They can occur in any order, all at once, or repeat themselves until the desired change has been made.

- Understand first
- Identify your goal
- Define action steps
- Teach each other
- Refine the process

To help understand the process of change, we will define each of these components one-by-one and then use two examples to demonstrate how they work together to create positive changes.

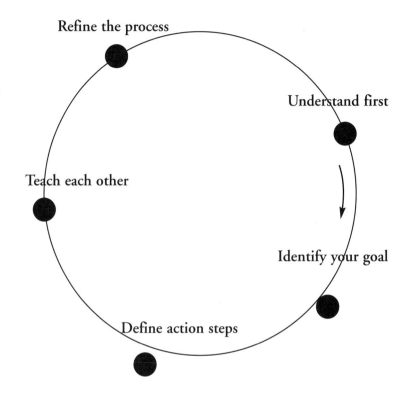

Understand First

The first component in the process of change is to understand first. We have discussed this communication skill in depth in previous chapters. Seeking to genuinely understand your partner by using paraphrasing and clarifying questions, along with congruent communication skills, will go a long way towards creating change.

Identify Your Goal

Through the process of understanding first, a clear goal will need to be established. This requires you to take an us-versus-the-problem approach so that you are on the same side. It also requires you to compromise and accommodate each other in the process. It is very important that you both mutually agree on your goal. When creating change, it is often helpful to write down your goal. This makes it easier to remember what you are trying to accomplish and allows you to stay focused.

Define Action Steps

Once you know where you want to go, you will need to identify a means of getting there. What are you going to do differently in order to reach your goal? If your goal is to stop being a back-seat driver, what are you going to replace your old behavior with? Defining these action steps is crucial. Perhaps you decide that the next time you feel the urge to tell your partner how to drive, instead you will start laughing to yourself. Another distraction technique would be to look out the side window and silently count to ten. Without identifying these steps, it is easy to revert back to or maintain your old behavior. When this occurs, not only will you both be disappointed, but you will feel less confident, comfortable or willing to work together. Each time this happens, it becomes more and more difficult to resolve future challenges.

Teach Each Other

Once you have identified your goal and the standards or behaviors that you will change, then you have to teach each other how to make the change a reality. This is where so many couples get confused. What does it mean to teach each other? In Chapter One, "Understanding and Respecting Your Relationship," we discussed how you are both a teacher and a student. Because of this, you and your partner are always influencing and being influenced by one another. Therefore, your actions can teach each other new behaviors, or they can reinforce old habits and patterns. Perhaps the best way to teach each other, once you have defined your goal and action steps, is through positive reinforcement.

There are entire books dedicated to the concept of positive reinforcement, but the idea is simple. When properly applied, positive reinforcement increases the likelihood that the behavior will be repeated. Showing appreciation and respect for your partner's successes and failures will be encouraging and motivating.

Use positive reinforcement whenever a positive step is made, no matter how big or small. When you reach an agreement or decision, thank each other. Acknowledge the commitment and hard work of each other, regardless of how smooth or difficult the process was. We need to feel validated when we are doing something right, and positive reinforcement accomplishes this swiftly.

One of the biggest mistakes couples make is waiting for complete change before rewarding each other. The secret is in noticing the little things, showing praise with verbal and non-verbal acknowledgements such as a smile, a soft touch, or a sincere "thank you." Identifying a goal is easy; but teaching each other what the behaviors associated with the goal feel and act like takes time. I have met few individuals who do not respond well to positive recognition. We all need to receive confirmation that we are on the right track far before we arrive at our destination. When we have fallen off track, a positive gesture can also go a long way. For instance, take the following response by Cindy after her boyfriend, Dave, gets off track and starts to become negative.

Cindy: *It's okay; I understand you're frustrated. We all have bad days.*

Dave: *I have had a bad day and I want to scream.*

Cindy: *Given everything that has happened today, you're doing great. Let's just slow down and start over.*

Dave: *That sounds good, but first I just need to scream.*

When you are already disappointed or frustrated, the last thing you need is negative attention. A little support and appreciation, such as indicated above, will put you back on your feet much more quickly than any unsupportive gesture.

There are "windows of opportunity" in your relationship when your partner is more susceptible to your influences. These moments in time are great opportunities to provide positive reinforcement to your partner's thoughts, feelings and actions. Many couples try to influence one another without paying attention to their timing. This reduces their success because they are not taking advantage of the most teachable moments. After your spouse has had an unusually difficult day at work, it is not the best time to focus on how you need more help around the house. On the other hand, after your partner has helped out with a chore, it is a good time to use positive reinforcement and discuss how you can work together to keep up with the never ending task of cleaning the house.

When is your partner more open or close-minded? Pay attention to "windows of opportunity" and take advantage of these teachable moments by using positive reinforcement to move your relationship to a better place.

Refine the Process

Creating change is a continuous process of evaluating what is working and what is not. By taking the time to refine the process, you take the opportunity to reinforce each other by understanding first, clarifying your goals and actions, as well as acknowledging your accomplishments. Without going through this step, you would be leaving things unclear and would certainly decrease your chances of reaching your desired change. Through the process of refining, you get a chance to clarify your actual goal. For instance, your initial goal may have been to communicate more effectively, but after review, it may simply come down to being more respectful and honest with each other. This clarification allows you to further define your action steps and allows you to support each other towards the desired change.

Here are some questions you can ask yourself and each other when you are refining the process.

- ❏ How have we reached our goal?
- ❏ Where have we been successful?
- ❏ Where have we not been successful?
- ❏ What do I/we need to do more/less of?
- ❏ How can we be more supportive?

Creating Change

Now that we have reviewed the various steps in the process of change, let's look at how they come together. To illustrate this, we will walk through two fictitious examples. The first is a recurring problem between Theresa and Joe, who continually get caught in a downward cycle of being critical, demanding and sarcastic with one another. The second is an example of how a couple used the process of change to resolve their back-seat driver tensions.

The downward cycle of being critical, demanding and sarcastic

<u>Understand first:</u> Through understanding each other, Joe and Theresa come to the following conclusion: Joe is sarcastic when he is frustrated with Theresa, and she in return becomes very defensive and demanding. The more defensive she becomes, the more sarcastic he is in response.

<u>Identify goal:</u> Theresa and Joe recognize that all they really want is to be more supportive of each other. They know that by overcoming the negative pattern they have created in their relationship, much tension and frustration will be released.

<u>Define action steps:</u> Joe and Theresa agree that they want to be more supportive of each other and need to do things differently. But what, exactly, are they going to do differently? Together, they decide that instead of Joe being sarcastic, he

needs to open up and share his thoughts and feelings in a productive manner before getting frustrated and becoming sarcastic. To accomplish this, Joe decides that whenever he starts to feel like he is losing emotionally he will stop whatever he is doing (use a distraction technique) by holding his hands out in front of him while wiggling his fingers. Once he is refocused, he can then share what he is feeling and why. On the other hand, Theresa needs to become less demanding and more accepting when Joe does not complete every task to her personal standards. To accomplish this she decides to let go of some of her preferences.

<u>Teach each other:</u> They have agreed that Joe is going to start sharing more before his frustration level builds, and Theresa is going to be more accepting of Joe. To accomplish this task, Joe needs to teach Theresa how to be less demanding and more accepting, and Theresa needs to teach Joe how to be less sarcastic. To be successful, both Joe and Theresa will need to recognize and acknowledge each other's efforts. This process will not be easy, as both will have a strong desire to revert to their old behavior only because it is more familiar.

In their last argument, Joe appropriately restrained his sarcasm for a few minutes, but quickly fell back into his comfort zone and started being sarcastic. Which of the following responses from Theresa would be the most encouraging to Joe?

A. *There you go, being all sarcastic again. I told you, you will never change!*
B. *Joe, you are becoming sarcastic.*
C. *Joe, I know you are trying hard. But you are becoming sarcastic, and I feel myself getting defensive.*

Response "A" will clearly pull this couple back into their negative pattern. Response "B" is a move in the right direction, but response "C" is the most supportive of Joe's efforts and allows Theresa to acknowledge her feelings and emotions as well.

Joe's response to Theresa is equally important. Remember, he is trying to teach Theresa to be less critical and more supportive. Consider the following dialogue:

Theresa: *Joe, you're becoming sarcastic, and I feel myself getting defensive!*

Joe's possible responses:
A. *Whatever!*
B. *Okay!*
C. *Thanks for not jumping all over me. I am trying.*

Clearly response "C" will teach and reinforce Theresa, as well as, continue to build a more supportive relationship between Joe and Theresa.

Refine the process: Theresa and Joe decide to sit down every month and discuss their successes and failures in creating the changes they want. Through their discussions, each feels the other is trying and taking the time to acknowledge positive steps. They also learn in this process that they are both a little too sensitive to each other's thoughts and feelings and need to focus on being more confident with themselves. They also identify the need to be more congruent with their communication skills and recognize when they are losing emotionally, so they can turn the situation around before it gets out of hand. These clarifications allow them to forge ahead more clearly towards their goal.

The back-seat driver

To some extent, we are all back seat drivers, but for this example, let us review how the process of change helps John and Marie manage their back-seat driving problem. In this case, John really is an aggressive driver—he rides the tail lights of the car ahead of him and makes quick lane changes without a blinker. Marie, on the other hand, is a courteous driver who proceeds with a flare of caution, always using her turn signals and making smooth lane changes. The challenge this couple faces is obvious. John's driving leads Marie to be scared and anxious, while Marie's driving leads John to become frustrated. As a result, regardless of who is driving, tension exists between them.

As you can imagine, this couple has tried to resolve this problem many times before, but time and time again the only thing that happens is that they both end up frustrated and with headaches. The primary reason for this is their inability to use basic communication skills. Instead, they get caught in their emotions and quickly fall off track as they defend their positions and force their points. For example:

Marie:	*When you drive, my heart sometimes pounds I am so scared.*
John:	*Don't worry so much. I have not been in an accident in over ten years.*
Marie:	*You drive too fast and need to slow down!*
John:	*No, I do not. I know what I am doing. I am in control!*

You can quickly see that Marie and John need to get refocused. They need to acknowledge each other's thoughts and feelings by *understanding first*. To achieve this, they will need to focus on paraphrasing and clarifying questions until each of them feels fully understood.

Marie: *When you drive, my heart sometimes pounds I am so scared. You drive so close to other cars and accelerate at the slightest opportunity to pass.*

John: *You're not comfortable with my driving?*

Marie: *No, I am afraid you're going to cause an accident or even worse—hurt someone.*

John: *I am not going to hurt anyone.*

Marie: *I know, but if you could just back off a little, I would be more comfortable.*

John: *Let me get this straight. If I did not drive so close to other cars, you would feel much safer. Is that correct?*

Marie: *Yes, that would make me feel much better. I would not be such a back-seat driver if I was more comfortable.*

John: *You mean you would not be jumping all over me?*

Marie: *My concerns would be greatly reduced, yes.*

John: *I do not feel that my driving is that bad.*

Marie: *How do you perceive you are driving?*

John: *I believe most people are indecisive and will cause accidents because they are too cautious. Therefore, I drive defensively.*

Marie: *So you drive more aggressively to be safer?*

John: *Yes.*

As this process continues, John and Marie begin to understand and acknowledge each other for the first time. Once they reach a mutual point of understanding, they can decide what to do with this new information.

John: *So, we are very different drivers, and we both get frustrated with each other due to every thing we have discussed. What do you think we can*

> *do to resolve this problem?*
>
> Marie: *I believe there are many things we can do to reduce each other's tensions.*

By working together John and Marie are able to *identify a goal.*

> Marie: *Are we in agreement on what we will do?*
> John: *Yes, we will both ease up on our back seat driving.*
> Marie: *Okay, it's a deal!*

At this point, John and Marie have, for the first time, identified a mutual goal. Although they both feel good about reaching this point, nothing has changed. Marie is still a more cautious driver than John. To this point, 5% of their time has focused on a solution and 95% of their interactions have been complaining and arguing about each other's driving skills. Clearly, their habits and past experiences are still working against them at this juncture. However, for the first time they are on the same side and have a mutual goal. Now they need to identify what *action steps* they are going to take to change their behaviors. How are they going to ease up on their back seat driving? Together they decide that John will give at least four to five car lengths between his car and the car in front of him and use his blinkers. Mary agrees to reduce her distance down to eight to ten car lengths and to be more decisive with her lane changes. They both also agree that they will be more tolerant of each other's driving habits.

As you can tell, these actions are general in nature and it will not be until they start working on them that they will become further defined. For instance, after further discussions they decide that John's blinker should blink at least three times before he can make a lane change. Likewise, more decisive lane changes for Marie will mean two different things to them. They will need to further clarify this difference as well. Furthermore, what does it mean for them to be more tolerant of each other's driving habits? As these clarifications are being made they will need to work together *to teach, support and encourage each other* to adopt the behavior changes they have identified.

John:	*I just have to say, thanks for not jumping on me back there. I was all over that car and did not even realize it.*
Marie:	*I know, my heart started pounding, but I knew I had to hold back from telling you how to drive.*

Or

John:	*It must have been a little scary when that car pulled right out in front of you.*
Marie:	*Yes it was, but I held my cool and did not brake hard like I normally would.*
John:	*Great job!*

These types of interactions reinforce the change and the teamwork between Marie and John. By continuing this process, they are sure to create a new pattern in their driving habits. Unfortunately, things will not always go this smoothly. John is certain to have a bad day, be in a rush and lose his interest in driving more cautiously. Marie is going to have to ask herself, "Is this a window of opportunity?" If it is not, she may want to pass on this situation and instead focus on it next week when they review their progress. Similarly, there will be times when Marie's driving will be bothersome for John.

It is at this point that John and Marie need to take time to *refine the process.* By reviewing and clarifying their goal and actions they can continue to make positive strides. As each feels more comfortable with the topic of driving, they can push a little harder on each other. Eventually, Marie will be able to say, "John, you need to slow down!" Due to his retraining, he will not be defensive and will respond appropriately by slowing down. This is when you know you are on the path of success. Contrary to what most people think, you can be very direct with one another without receiving a defensive response, but this position is something you earn over time. Certainly the more interdependence that exists, the easier it becomes to reach this state.

You can see how using the various components of problem-solving, as part of the process of change, can help a couple break their challenge into more manageable pieces. Remember, there is no perfect order for the process of change to occur. Some challenges work themselves out quickly, while others take an incredible amount of energy just to reach an understanding. Typically, the harder it is for you to understand first, the more barriers you will face as you strive to support each other through the change. Do not let this prevent you from moving forward, continually refining and clarifying your goals and actions.

Clearly, the more emotionally-aware and interdependent you are, the easier the process of working with your partner becomes. Creating change does not only come from focusing on relationship issues. Many improvements can be made in your relationship by simply focusing on yourself. Preferences are a good example of this; the less emotional energy you expend on them, the more you will have to focus on what is most important to you.

SUMMARY POINTS

Change is not an event; it is a process. As you become more familiar with the steps for creating change, your confidence will build and your problems will no longer represent barriers. Instead, they will become opportunities to learn and grow together. Use the process of change as a catalyst for breaking patterns and building stronger connections with your partner.

Self-Assessment Questions:
- ❏ What challenges recur in our relationship?
- ❏ What is the difference between problem-solving and creating change?
- ❏ Which step in the process of change am I most uncomfortable with?
- ❏ What can I do to support my partner more during the process of change?

Moving Forward

Using the process of change is a crucial element in choosing to build a successful relationship. The next chapter will continue to show you how to overcome barriers by turning your relationship challenges into opportunities. As you accomplish this you will further enhance your ability to make right turns in your relationship.

CHAPTER ELEVEN

Turning Your Challenges into Opportunities

"Things do not change, we do."
—Henry David Thoreau

All relationships are faced with challenges and certainly your relationship is no different. As a matter of fact, if your relationship does not experience tension and strain, from time to time, you should be concerned. In a healthy relationship, challenges play an important role. They give you and your partner the opportunity to understand and learn from each other. If this process is effectively managed, you will feel valued, respected and appreciated, all of which will allow you to manage future challenges more easily and effectively. If the process is not effectively managed, you will quickly find yourself feeling a host of unsupportive emotions that will not help you resolve your existing or future challenges.

What challenges (barriers) do you face in your relationship? Take a minute to identify ongoing challenges in your relationship that need to be resolved.

Ongoing challenges in our relationship.
1. _____
2. _____
3. _____
4. _____
5. _____
6. _____
7. _____
8. _____
9. _____
10. _____

Guidelines for Turning Challenges into Opportunities

To help convert your challenges into opportunities, make sure to follow these guidelines:

- Focus on one barrier at a time
- Make sure you mutually agree
- If you agree to it, commit to it
- Let go of what is comfortable
- Avoid self-sabotage
- Focus on the process of creating change

By adhering to these guidelines, you will proactively take control of your relationship's future, decrease the amount of unneeded tension, and build a stronger, more supportive relationship.

Focus on one barrier at a time

At any given time, you will want to focus on only one relationship challenge at a time. More is not better when it involves overcoming challenges. If you try to improve too many areas at one time, you will surely fail. As a matter of fact, you will want to start with the least difficult challenge you face, rather than with your biggest. Remember, it is better to be successful with smaller challenges than to start with your most emotional challenges and fail. To build your momentum, you need to establish a pattern of success. This momentum can then allow you to successfully manage greater challenges in your relationship.

Make sure you mutually agree

When creating a goal, you are establishing a new precedent, standard or expectation for both you and your partner. Like most things, these expectations are choices, and in order for them to be successful, they must be mutual decisions. If either of you is resistant or even hesitant to establish a specific expectation, then do not choose it, even though it is a problem area in your relationship. It is far more helpful to focus on areas you are both fully committed to and be successful, than it is to invest in something that you are not mutually focused on and fail. Over time, after overcoming several challenges, both you and your partner will become more comfortable with the process. As this happens, you will become mutually interested in resolving areas in which you were previously not.

If you agree to it, commit to it

Once an expectation has been mutually agreed upon, both you and your partner are responsible for holding to it. We have all committed to something half-heartedly such as losing weight or starting up a new exercise program. Such commitments can be short-lived and easily forgotten. This is not the case for these mutually-agreed-upon goals. They are convictions to your relationship and each other. When Lisa and I started resolving our challenges, we made absolute commitments to making them happen. Of course, we both also knew that neither of us could change just by talking. We recognized that we would both make mistakes; yet at the same time, we knew we were both committed to reaching our new expectations. This gave us the strength and patience to move forward during tough times. Eventually, we unlearned old behaviors and picked up new, more supportive habits. As you discuss what challenges you want to improve upon, make sure you and your partner are fully committed to the change. If either one of you is not, then pick a new challenge which you are both committed to resolving.

Let go of what is comfortable

It takes hard work and dedication to create personal change since many of our behaviors are automatic. For instance, do you think about how to drive each time you get behind the wheel? Certainly not; your thoughts and actions have been programmed over repeated exposure. This same type of programming takes place repeatedly in your daily interactions. Contrary to popular opinion, even the simplest change can create unknown resistance inside you. This is not because you do not want to change, but because you are accustomed to specific thoughts, feelings and behaviors. In order to be successful, we all have to learn to let go of what is comfortable. For example, if you typically hold in your thoughts and feelings, learning how to share them with your partner requires letting go of the comfort that comes from holding onto them. This requires leaving your normal and predictable behavior (what is comfortable and familiar) and trading it for something new (uncomfortable and unfamiliar). It is by building new connections that old ones fade away.

Avoid self-sabotage

For some reason, we are all good at sabotaging ourselves. This is attributed more to the power of our old habits than it is to intention. The desire to quit smoking can be genuine, but in certain situations the appeal for smoking becomes almost irresistible. Similarly, in our relationships, when things get tense, we have a tendency to default to automatic pilot. If we are used to being sarcastic to make our point, we will revert to this tactic when in the right situation. It is important to accept this as a normal part of the process. Therefore, when you revert to an old habit, be ready with a pattern breaker and don't allow yourself to get too far off track. Likewise, if your partner reverts, avoid going down the same road. Again, use a pattern breaker to reset both of your emotional states. Avoid self-sabotage by holding yourself accountable and choosing actions that support the changes you are committed to making.

Focus on the process of creating change

When focusing on overcoming a challenge, you are also most likely in need of creating behavior changes in each other. As we have discussed, this is not easy, but by working together to reach mutual goals, it is possible. You will need to rely on the skills and topics covered throughout this book. You will need to set aside preferences and set clear boundaries. You will need to focus on the positive and hold each other accountable. Most importantly, you have to create a safe environment by understanding first and learning how to support each other through the process of change. This means guiding and teaching each other as you both learn from your successes and failures.

Reviewing your progress towards your new standards and expectations keeps them fresh in your mind and reinforces their value. A focused mind is a powerful ally. Set time aside to review this progress. Initially this should be done weekly, then slowly progress to monthly, quarterly and yearly as you become successful in overcoming challenges. When you review your progress, focus on your successes first. Take pride in the hard work both of you are doing and the things you have accomplished. This revitalizes your relationship and reinforces your commitment to each other. When reviewing the areas not being met, do not get too uptight the first few times. Be patient, yet persistent. It's okay if some of your goals take longer to accomplish. The world does not change in a day and neither will your relationship. Just keep pushing forward and learning from your mistakes. This determination and accountability will drive you towards the changes you seek to accomplish.

I do not mean to make this process sound too easy. From my own experiences, observing and talking with other couples, there are many times we want to give up and do. Sometimes, just when things are getting better, you or your partner might make a mistake or lose patience, either of which can be emotionally draining. This is where emotional awareness and interdependence can really help communication and problem-solving skills as you seek to overcome relationship challenges.

Next, we will review several challenges that Lisa and I faced in our relationship. The hope is that these personal examples will clarify how the many skills we have talked about come together and how they can also turn your relationship challenges into opportunities.

Turning Challenges into Opportunities

Several years ago, Lisa and I had come to an impasse, and realized that our relationship was not going to be successful unless we resolved our ongoing challenges. Rather than give up, we decided to resolve our relationship challenges once and for all. To get us back on track, we identified the specific long-standing challenges that needed to be resolved. These challenges included poor listening skills, going to bed mad, bringing up old issues and not being supportive of each other.

Resolving these challenges proved to be an arduous task.

It required us to understand first, problem-solve and create change, all of which truly tested our emotional awareness, communication skills, level of interdependence, as well as our preferences, negotiables and boundaries.

As with any change, we were not immediately successful in our efforts. In many cases, it was not our communication skills that held us together; it was our commitment to our new expectations and each other that did. We had to work hard to convert our existing challenges into opportunities. However, over time, we were able to, and as each issue was resolved, the tension between us diminished, and we had more energy for rewarding activities. The process Lisa and I had to go through and will continue to go through is no different than the ongoing process that all couples experience in order to be successful.

Below are four different challenges Lisa and I mutually agreed to overcome in our relationship. We will discuss the first of these four challenges in-depth to demonstrate how healthy communication and problem-solving skills work together to overcome a relationship challenge. The last three examples will be briefly covered to further demonstrate the types of challenges that, once resolved, can bring immediate satisfaction to a relationship.

- Poor listening skills
- Going to bed mad
- Bringing up old issues
- Being unsupportive

You can see, from the list above, we did not listen with open minds, we went to bed mad too often, when frustrated we brought up past issues, and we did not consistently support each other in our decisions. To some extent, it was amazing that we had not given up a long time ago. We were and are far from perfect, but had we chosen to give up and end our relationship, as couples so often do, we would have been faced with many similar, as well as, many different challenges in our next relationships. There is no perfect partner or relationship. The success of any relationship is up to the couple.

Relationship Barrier #1: Poor listening skills

Our ineffective communication was the first challenge that Lisa and I needed to overcome. Overall, we had very different communication styles. She processed her thoughts and feelings internally and required time to think things through before sharing. I was the exact opposite; I processed and verbalized my thoughts and feelings quickly. As you can imagine, this created a huge barrier between us. When discussing an important issue, our differences would collide. With each passing moment, as I waited for Lisa to respond to a question, the more frustrated I grew. The more frustrated I grew, the more anxious she became and the less comfortable she was with sharing. This vicious cycle played out time and time again between us. It left us angry, frustrated, and disappointed and the problem unresolved.

We had both been trained well and were very comfortable with our existing communication styles. My family is loud; we talk fast, state our opinions, get emotional and even have a tendency to talk over one another. This is the exact opposite in Lisa's family. Conversations are quieter, non-confrontational and they do not have a tendency to talk all at the same time.

We both wanted the other to behave as we were most accustomed to. Neither of us meant any harm, but we had different expectations. Eventually, we recognized that regardless of the difference in our styles, neither of us was a better communicator, and we needed to work together to communicate successfully. Therefore, our goal was to improve our communication process so that we both felt we were working on the same team. Recognizing and accepting our current habits were huge steps toward understanding where we were trying to go and what we needed to do.

To move forward, I had to learn how to be more patient, talk less and wait for a response. Lisa had to learn to take risks and share her thoughts and feelings more openly. These tasks were equally daunting for both of us. We needed to learn from each other and adapt if we were to achieve our new expectations. In order to be successful, we had to teach each other how to acquire these skills. It was not until I started trying to wait patiently for an answer that I fully recognized that anything over a second was a long time for me to wait. Slowly, but surely, I began to understand how my behavior could easily appear demanding.

Breaking old patterns (habits) is not easy. I had to learn to pace myself and show a little patience. One trick I learned while driving was to count telephone poles. After I asked a question or stated my thoughts or feelings, I would count telephone poles as we passed them by. Counting acted as a distraction for me and provided Lisa time to think and respond. I believe the key to the success of this approach was in the positive reinforcement that followed. Lisa would thank me for giving her time to process her thoughts and feelings. This acknowledgement made me feel appreciated and encouraged me to be more patient.

Lisa, on the other hand, had to learn how to feel comfortable expressing herself. She would accomplish this in two ways. First, when I was impatient, she would acknowledge my efforts anyway. This meant that she was not retreating, but instead participating in the process. Second, she would take a risk by sharing her thoughts and feelings before reviewing them several times in her mind. Each time she did this, it was my responsibility to thank her for sharing, no matter how long it took to express her thoughts. Together, these behaviors increased her comfort level by making her feel safe to express her thoughts and feelings. As you can see, our focus was on ourselves, and also on teaching and reinforcing each other.

Through our efforts Lisa and I were able to eliminate much of the emotional tension that developed between us while in discussions. Rather than getting stuck or pulled off track because of our communication differences, we began listening to and understanding each other at a much more effective level. This made sharing our different opinions, feelings or needs safer than ever before. Some topics are not easy to discuss, and had we not gone through this process of change together, we are positive many discussions would have been avoided altogether and many others would have only made things worse.

Initially, every few months Lisa and I reviewed our communication successes and failures and reinforced our efforts to work together to meet our goals. Now we are so comfortable with our current process that this past barrier requires very little attention. Through this refining process we were able to recognize and reinforce our commitment to working together. It certainly took us time and several failures to overcome our communication barrier, but as a result we were able to dramatically improve our relationship.

Relationship Barrier #2: Going to bed mad

For some time we had what we considered a bad habit. Rather than identifying and dealing with issues when they arose, we would go to bed upset. Even worse, we would avoid issues afterwards as if they had magically disappeared. It did not take us long to realize that old, unresolved issues would come back to bite us. Neither of us intentionally tried to hurt one another; however, we were good at it. When we realized that we both needed improvement in this area, we vowed to overcome this relationship challenge. Taking this step forced us to address our problems before they got away from us. We also learned that some challenges are too big to be fully resolved in one night. In these situations, we agreed to continue the discussion the following day or as long as it took to find a resolution. This also allowed us time to reflect on the issue at hand and more effectively communicate and seek a solution the following day. Suddenly, rather than brewing about problems for weeks, we were addressing and resolving them in days. As a result, we saved a great deal of negative energy and prevented many small challenges from growing out of proportion. This single change made an immediate positive impact on our relationship.

Relationship Barrier #3: Bringing up old issues

In the past, if either of us felt vulnerable or angry, we used old issues as a shield to defend ourselves emotionally. In essence, we would not let go of past mistakes. This coping mechanism was unhealthy and created more problems than it was worth, so we decided it was no longer acceptable to treat each other this way. This decision was very important and has allowed us to deal with the facts in front of us rather than being undermined by past situations. Disagreements can be hard enough to manage without adding fuel to the fire. Overcoming this barrier proved challenging, but the process raised our emotional awareness to a new more rewarding level.

Relationship Barrier #4: Being unsupportive

Lisa and I have had to make many choices together and for a long time, if things did not work out as expected, one or both of us would complain. For instance, we would go out to dinner and then complain about the bad service or food. To make matters worse, if one of us really did not want to go to the restaurant in the first place, that one would blame the other for the decision. This pattern was very unsupportive, so we decided that whenever "we" make a choice, "we" would both make the best of it, whether this was a vacation, a night on the town or a new purchase. This expectation has simplified our life and turned otherwise boring or frustrating situations into something enjoyable. Now, if we go to a restaurant and the food or service is not to our expectations, we enjoy ourselves anyway.

Making Forward Progress

Focusing on your relationship's challenges is an easy way to identify where you both lack skills and need to set new expectations. Perhaps the biggest key to any couple's success is learning how to teach and support each other through the process of change. As you successfully turn challenges into opportunities, you will experience a great amount of satisfaction. There are very few things more rewarding than knowing that you have overcome a challenge together. This not only soothes the soul, but it also builds your confidence in yourself and your partner. When times are tough you need to believe in yourself just as much as you need to believe in your partner. With each additional success comes more confidence and, as this momentum builds, your fears, hesitations or concerns related to overcoming barriers will greatly diminish.

SUMMARY POINTS

Turning your challenges into opportunities will be more easily accomplished by following the guidelines we reviewed. You have identified a list of areas you want to improve upon in your relationship. Start working on them one at a time. The greatest benefit of overcoming your existing relationship barriers is that, in doing so, you actually become better prepared to resolve future challenges. This is important as, over time, your needs, wants, expectations and circumstances will change. As a result, you will be faced with numerous new challenges to resolve. It is not necessary for these to be perceived as barriers. Instead they should be avenues for personal growth and facilitate the long-term success of your relationship.

Self-Assessment Questions:
- ❑ How have we established mutual areas of growth?
- ❑ How do we support each other towards our goals?
- ❑ What has prevented us from successfully overcoming challenges in the past?
- ❑ What past challenges have we been successful in overcoming and why?

Moving Forward

Now that we have discussed how to turn your challenges into opportunities, the rest is up to you. The final chapter, "Creating an Action Plan," is a brief summary of what we have discussed thus far, and it challenges you to create a plan for making right turns in your relationship.

CHAPTER TWELVE

Creating an Action Plan

"Coming together is a beginning;
keeping together is a process;
working together is success."

—Henry Ford

W e have covered a variety of ideas throughout this book.
As we progressed from chapter to chapter, these ideas
built upon one another, demonstrating together the complex
factors that determine the overall state of your relationship.
Because of your relationship's complexity, it can be difficult to
sort through all of this information and use it to your relationship's advantage. The best way of overcoming this obstacle is by creating an action plan to help guide your future
actions. To facilitate this process, make sure your action plan
includes the following components, each of which is sure to
move you in the right direction.

✓ Take advantage of your relationship's strengths
✓ Reinvest in your past successes
✓ Prioritize your areas for improvement
✓ Create a relationship rule book

Each of these steps plays a vital role in your action plan,
but it is their combined effectiveness that truly makes a positive impact on your relationship.

Take Advantage of Your Relationship's Strengths

There are many things you and your partner are doing right in your relationship. For instance, you may do a good job managing preferences, paraphrasing or investing in quality time with each other. Whatever these strengths, it is important that you acknowledge and continue them into the future. One of the best ways to acknowledge your relationship's strengths is to identify and share them with your partner (as you did in Chapter Three). This action reinforces your confidence and in turn increases the likelihood of these behaviors continuing.

Strengths that you want to continue in your relationship.

1. _____
2. _____
3. _____
4. _____
5. _____

It is so easy to become over focused on what's not going right that we often forget what is going right in our relationship. To avoid this trap, make sure you take the time to recognize and acknowledge what is going well in your relationship. Show appreciation and support for each other whenever you can. Take advantage of every opportunity to make your partner feel special.

Reinvest in Your Past Successes

More likely than not, you have discontinued some behaviors that were once positive influences in your relationship. This could have been something as simple as buying flowers, going for walks together or snuggling up in bed. Whatever these old behaviors were, they can be re-initiated with far less effort than it takes to start a new habit. Give yourself some easy successes by rejuvenating those activities that once brought satisfaction to your relationship.

Positive behaviors that you want to reinstate in your relationship.
1. _____
2. _____
3. _____
4. _____
5. _____

We all want to start new habits in our relationship that we believe will improve our level of satisfaction. Personal experience, however, shows us that it is not always easy to start a new habit. Therefore, it is important that you take advantage of your past successes and relish the satisfaction that comes from acting on them once again.

Prioritize Your Areas for Improvement

Once you have taken advantage of your relationship strengths and re-established past positive behaviors then it is time to focus on specific areas for improvement.

Where are your opportunities for improvement? Have you reached the level of interdependence you seek? Do you feel your level of emotional awareness is an asset to your relationship? Do you make your relationship a priority by investing in it on a consistent basis? Are your personal rules controlling you or are you controlling them? Are your communication skills supporting your goals? How would you rate your ability to understand first? Do you have a clear relationship vision? When it comes to problem-solving, creating change and working together, do you not only understand these processes, but do you use them to your advantage?

On the chart below, identify which chapter topics need improvement in your relationship and which do not. Then prioritize those topics that need improvement, by ranking them in order of importance (1, 2, 3...).

Chapter Topics	Does not need focus	Needs focus	Rank of importance (1,2,3...)
Your Relationship Vision			
Making Your Relationship a Priority			
Creating Interdependence			
Emotional Awareness			
The Rules You Live By			
Communication			
Understand First			
Problem-Solving			
Creating Change			
Turning Your Challenges into Opportunities			

Completing this exercise will give you an understanding of where to focus your time and energy. Now the only question is where to start? If you're like most couples there are several topics on which you could focus your attention. In the best interest of success, avoid working on multiple topics. When too many topics are focused on at once, couples often feel overwhelmed, confused and ineffective. This can lead to frustration and a sense of hopelessness. I also recommend you avoid focusing on your most difficult areas first. For many couples this is a natural inclination, but in taking this approach there is an increased chance for failure. Therefore, one of the most effective approaches is to start with those areas which provide the least amount of resistance and offer the greatest chances of success.

Certainly, we all want to problem-solve effectively, create healthy changes and overcome our relationship challenges. These are all topics covered in the last three chapters, but your success in managing them will depend on how well you have developed the skills discussed in earlier chapters. As you begin to take on the more challenging tasks in your relationship seriously consider creating a relationship rule book.

Create a Relationship Rule Book

To help address our challenges, Lisa and I created what we coined, "our rule book." This is a small notebook in which we identified our relationship challenges. We then mutually-agreed to improve our challenges, one at a time, until they were each resolved. Writing these down allowed us to establish guiding principles and clear expectations for our relationship and each other. The ground rules to creating a rule book are simple.

1. Only identify challenges which you mutually-agree to resolve.
2. Only focus on improving one challenge at a time. Once you have been successful in creating a positive change, then you can start working on another one.
3. Review your rule book on a regular basis.

Lisa and I have found our rule book to be a stabilizer in our relationship. The first opportunities for improvement we wrote in our rule book were: improving our listening skills, not going to bed mad, not bringing up old issues and being more supportive of our individual and collective decisions. Today, we continue to use our rule book to direct the success of our relationship. We also review it on a regular basis and reflect on the positive changes we have made together.

Many couples start their rule book by writing their relationship vision. This seems to get them focused. Then they start identifying mutually-agreeable opportunities for improvement. There is no reason to make your rule book a huge list of standards and expectations. It is not intended to be an exhaustive list. Instead, it focuses on the main objectives you want to improve upon in your relationship. After more than a decade of using our rule book, Lisa and I have only identified twenty items (opportunities for improvement) and it is unlikely that we will come up with another ten. More is not necessarily better when it comes to your rule book, as you do not want to get caught up in preferences.

SUMMARY POINTS

To make right turns in your relationship, knowing where to focus your efforts will be of tremendous assistance. In doing so, you increase your chances of successfully reaching your relationship vision. First and foremost, acknowledge those things that are already going well and continue them. Second, re-establish old healthy habits which had previously brought you and your partner happiness, comfort and pleasure. Finally, make sure you have prioritized the key areas you need to improve upon in yourself and your relationship.

Certainly no person or relationship is perfect; however, there is no substitute for a good action plan to give you clear direction and focus. Combine this action plan with a little persistence and determination and almost anything can happen.

Self-Assessment Questions:
- ❏ How am I taking advantage of our relationship's strengths?
- ❏ How am I re-initiating past positive actions?
- ❏ How have we prioritized our opportunities for improvement?
- ❏ What is our relationship's action plan?

Moving Forward

Lisa and I are no different than most couples. We have faced many struggles and opportunities in our relationship. We have also experienced a wealth of good times. However, the future success of any relationship, whether it is yours or ours, will be determined by the ability and willingness to bring two separate sets of perceptions, beliefs, values and cultures together into a common, mutually-shared system that supports the needs, wants and expectations of each partner.

Now it is up to you. What direction are you going to take your relationship? Certainly you have the necessary information to get you moving in the right direction, but please do not stop here. Every year you will learn more about your relationship, your partner and yourself. There will be new ground to cover. Develop within yourself and your relationship the skills necessary to manage future challenges, and turn them into opportunities for personal growth. Create a safe environment that fosters respect, appreciation and trust.

Whatever plan of action you choose, write it down, review your progress and clarify your goals by using the skills discussed throughout this book. Most importantly, remain flexible as you work together. Do not get lost in the process of change. If your current approach is not working, try something different until you find an approach that moves you towards your intended goal. Ultimately, this will enable you to establish a relationship in which:

> *"Independence is equal*
> *dependence is mutual*
> *and the obligation reciprocal."*
> —*Louis K. Anspacher*

Myron Lewis, M.S.W., is a dynamic speaker and writer with a passion for teaching couples how to excel in their relationships. He has a Master degree in Social Work from Western Michigan University and a Bachelor degree in Psychology from Michigan State University. Myron developed and has been teaching his couples communication seminar "Making Right Turns in Your Relationship" for more than a decade and has had the privilege of helping scores of individuals and couples improve the quality of their relationships. Mr. Lewis has been married for ten years to his wife, Lisa, and they have two beautiful daughters.

HANSYD PUBLISHING - ORDER FORM

Fax orders   (231) 242-0682

Postal orders   Hansyd Publishing
P.O. Box 557
Harbor Springs, MI 49740

On-line orders hansydpublishing.com

Please send me _____ copies of *Making Right Turns in Your Relationship*. Cost is $16.95 each, plus shipping and handling.

Name:_____

Address:_____

City:_____ State:_____ Zip Code:_____

Telephone:(____)_____

Email address:_____

Sales Tax: Please add 6% for products shipped to Michigan addresses.

Shipping: US: $4.00 for first book and $2.00 for each additional book.

Payment type: ❏ Check-enclosed   ❏ Credit Card

Credit Card #:_____

❏ Visa   ❏ Mastercard

Name on card:_____ Exp. Date:_____

Making *Right* Turns in Your Relationship